Million Dollar Plan

LEVERAGING TECHNOLOGY TO SCALE

Matthew J. Ganzak

SCALEUP MEDIA

NAPLES, FL

Matthew Ganzak / ScaleUP Media
8805 Tamiami Trail North
Suite #183
Naples, Florida 34108
matt@scaleupmedia.com

Ordering Information:
Quantity sales. Special discounts are available on quantity purchases by corporations, associations, and others. For details, contact the "Special Sales Department" at the address above.

Million Dollar Plan / Matthew J. Ganzak —1st ed.
ISBN 978-0-692-65457-6

CONTENTS

Dedicated to entrepreneurs who refuse to quit

He who is not courageous enough to take risks will accomplish nothing in life.
— MUHAMMAD ALI

INTRODUCTION

I am an average guy. Average in almost every way. I do not have famous parents. I was not a great student, I rarely stayed focused and I am not a superhero. I quit college after two years, failed ninth-grade English and my high school guidance counselor told me, "You will never amount to anything."

My financial situation was less than stellar, too. I was once evicted from my rental apartment because I could not afford the $300 a month rent.

When I could not pay my mortgage, my house was sold by short sale.

I couldn't afford to eat and had to choose between keeping the lights on or paying my water bill.

I have worked a dozen dead-end jobs with horrible bosses and spent years of my life just skating by.

We all go through problems; some problems are bigger than others.

One night as I was struggling to fall asleep because I was hungry, I promised myself that I would do whatever it took to change my situation.

I took ownership in my situation and decided to change my life. I walked away from dead-end jobs, and started building a sustainable future for myself and my family. This book takes you through the steps to create business and life you love. And will assist you with planning your future and your business.

AGAINST THE GRAIN

In high school, every student in my class had to take a standardized career placement test. I don't recall the results of my test, but I knew that I wanted to do something that was not on the standard list of potential careers.

I was a 3.0 student, with all honors classes and overall a bright kid. I would take tests without studying and base my answers solely on logic. If I had no interest in something, I just didn't do it. I was stubborn.

I had no idea what I wanted to do in life, but knew that I was different than the other students in my high school.

The year was 2001, and I remember the parent and teacher meeting quite vividly. Instead of working to develop my mind and powerful personality, I was told by my guidance counselor to drop out of high school and get a trade, like working on cars or being a bartender.

My parents, both successful entrepreneurs, introduced me to personal development in the form of books and audio recordings by Anthony Robbins, Jim Rohn and Jack Canfield. Without personal development, I might be working on cars in a garage or bartending, instead of achieving my dreams and goals and unlocking my full potential.

Know that we all have to start somewhere. It doesn't matter if you fail freshman English, like I did; know that you can still achieve your dreams regardless of what your teachers think of you.

Along the way, you will receive good and bad advice. But always remember to follow your dreams and never let anyone tell you that you cannot accomplish your goals.

WE ALL START SOMEWHERE

Ten years ago I started on my journey to build a successful business, and along the way endured success and failure. Most entrepreneurs would have given up by now. If I gave up, then you would not be reading this book. The crazy thing is that I have had all the tools for success at my fingertips for years, and I did not take the leap to get started. I was always making excuses.

I have been afraid of failure and, in some way, also scared of success. In some ways many of us fear the unknown, and success was beyond my safety net.

But beyond my fears, the number one success killer had its grip on my ambitions: procrastination. I would say to myself, "What do you expect from a 21-year-old?" That's exactly why I am writing this now at the age of 32.

There were excuses galore! I always had a new excuse - something always came up, or someone is distracting me. Or worse yet, the Internet has had its grip on my life since the 90s. Funny, even as I am writing this, I have to unplug from the Internet in order to get the words onto paper.

TAKE MASSIVE ACTION

Over the past 10 years, I've spent thousands of hours and hundreds of thousands of dollars in testing to find the shortest path to success. Inside I have carefully crafted each chapter to break down the Million Dollar Plan. I have used the fundamentals of this plan with every client and built seven-figure companies.

In 2004, I knew I wanted to help businesses with online marketing and website development, but I had no idea what a startup was. I was lost. And back then, Search Engine Optimization seemed like witchcraft to me. I was using Photoshop and Dreamweaver to create websites, which was taking forever! I was clueless!

Before I learned how to code properly, I was designing every page of a website from scratch in Photoshop and then exporting tables to HTML. If you remember these days, then you might remember how frustrating web development was early on. If you have no idea what I am talking about, consider yourself lucky.

Building a web business is just like building a house. If you build your house on sand, without a strong foundation, your house will eventually collapse under the weight. Building a sturdy foundation can allow you to skip starting over later down the road.

Ten years ago, while I was learning website development, I was charging what I had thought my time was worth. In fact, a few of my early projects were done for free. But after one success, I started charging a little more and then a little more. Eventually, I began charging for consultations, and I began to start respecting my time. Because I learned how valuable my time is worth.

Use this book as a tool to build the foundation of your new business and with the right mindset, you will eventually own a million-dollar company.

STARTING A BUSINESS IS DIFFICULT

Eight out of 10 new entrepreneurs who start businesses will fail in the first 18 months. Yet, there are entrepreneurs who start dozens of successful businesses in the same time period. Why?

How can two business people with similar resources have opposite results?

Entrepreneurs who have created one successful business can duplicate that success again and again. Every entrepreneur should start his or her company with a positive mindset. These positive waves are sent through employees, contractors, clients and partners to create future business success. This energy, as it builds the foundation of a new company, will assist with the difficult times in business. And difficult times are almost guaranteed with a new business.

Successful entrepreneurs also understand the fundamentals of creating a unique value proposition for their businesses and how to position their new companies in the marketplace for success. The Internet has made starting a new business cheaper and easier, but this results in more competition. Entrepreneurs need to learn who their customers are, what they are looking for, how to attract them and how to convince them (in less than one minute) why they should buy from their companies.

After creating a unique experience, visitors need to be engaged up to six additional times before a majority of sales will be made. It is not easy to create a captive audience, standing by at their computers with credit card in hand. It is especially hard for those who have never created online sales before. There are secrets to engaging users through social media, emails and customer service to seed the sale. Capturing, engaging and building brand loyalty are the keys to building a successful business. The secret is creating raving, loyal fans.

The best example of a raving fan can be seen in Apple fanatics. Customers, including myself, who are so excited about the newest product launch that we tune into the announcements of the new products on launch day. Eyes are glued to the screen as the product is unveiled. Then we reach for our wallets, happily inputting our credit card into web pages to buy the new shiny object. Apple has created millions of loyal customers who will always be clientele.

Once the business owner learns the formula to brand loyalty, success becomes easier to achieve. But how is this loyalty achieved? In this book, we will explore how to achieve creating sales and secrets to building repeat customers. First, we need to get started building the online presence and create the first sales for the new business.

Build. Test. Track. Repeat. Your website or promotions do not end once your business is built. This book explains how to test promotions, track results and then repeat tests. No two businesses will have the same marketing results, but in this book I will give you the formula for A/B testing and tracking the success or failure of promotions.

WHO IS THIS BOOK FOR?

This book was created with the novice entrepreneur in mind, while also creating value for advanced entrepreneurs. You could be developing a product, working to get your product online, or maybe your product or service is already online and it is not selling. You will find something in here that will help you.

I work with brick and mortar businesses and strictly online businesses. My training can help anyone from a lawyer or doctor or restaurant owner, to a blogger or app creator or someone who has an idea and is trying to get your dream online. In fact, I have worked with celebrities, musicians and authors! It doesn't matter who you are or what you are doing, I am positive that you can take something from this to apply to your business.

HOW THIS BOOK HELPS

In order to build a sustainable business, it is important to stay informed on the current marketing trends. Become an early adopter of new technology and beat your competitors to market. Arm yourself with the knowledge of Internet marketing and embrace the future ideas that will transform your business success.

Starting my professional career as an on-air radio personality, I believed that I was always going to work in radio and broadcasting. I enjoyed working with businesses by advertising and promoting events. In 2004, I was building simple websites for clients, but if you had told me then that I would be a successful web advisor later in life, I would have said you are crazy!

Technology has evolved since then. In a sense, I am still using my broadcasting talents through podcasting and my video training series online, but I vowed to always stay ahead of the trends in technology. This philosophy has contributed to a majority of my success today, and my formula for success is contained within these pages.

WHY AM I TELLING MY SECRETS?

One of my clients asked "Why do you give away all your secrets to making money online?" Now wait... don't roll your eyes. I am not one of those crazy "make $400 a day working from home" guys! Instead, I create websites for myself and my clients that get a ton of traffic. In fact, I have had over 1.6 million organic visits on my websites in a few months, all organic traffic!

Then I put up ads around my content and viola - ad revenue! I also have other websites that sell products, services and make money for my company, while working with clients to help their businesses achieve their goals while meeting their return of investment (ROI).

I have sold millions in products and services through my clients' businesses. I want to help you be successful, and the purpose of this book is to help you achieve your success. Understand that there is no shortcut to success. Maybe you can cut a corner and make a few dollars, but my training shows you how to build a sustaining business that will last!

This is not a get rich quick scheme, or some crazy claim that someone posted on your Facebook wall. This is my real life struggle to find what works and then I show you exactly how I accomplished success.

WHAT YOU WILL LEARN

This book will enable you to take my success and apply it to your business. Or if you are an expert at something, and you never thought of making a business from your expertise, I hope that you can have your ah-ha moment and get started building a business around something that you love.

I have dedicated the past 10 years as a student of successful entrepreneurs and testing methods to find what works. This training is the combination of thousands of dollars' worth of training and millions of dollars in A/B testing. In this book, I'm going to share with you the best marketing strategies that have helped me build multimillion dollar companies.

When I started my business, I had no idea what I was doing. I wanted to learn how to build a business, and no one was training on these best practices. These marketing strategies were not taught in schools, and there were no experts creating training like this online, so I was lost.

Fast forward 10 years to today, and while there are Internet marketing trainers, entrepreneurs are still lost when it comes to the execution of their ideas. Many of my clients read books and studied online courses, but then their ideas got stuck in neutral.

RISE ABOVE THE NOISE

Recently I became active in online entrepreneurial communities, where I have been offering free advice to those in need. It is astounding that there are so many free training programs with a wealth of knowledge online, yet so many are still stuck in neutral. Why?

It comes down to poor business planning, and so many people are trying to duplicate each other's success. There are far too many copycat entrepreneurs who understand how to put a website online, and how to get a new social media profile published. However, they miss the mark when it comes to identifying the market opportunity and fail to identify their target demographic.

Also, there are so many courses where experts are training on shortcuts and loopholes in the system, which, when exploited, can make money. Or, experts are training on how to use proprietary software and systems that are very narrowly focused towards building your business. If your business does not fit a specific mold, you could be lost.

INVEST IN YOUR EDUCATION

My clients want to build their businesses on a solid foundation, and they understand that their entrepreneurial education is the best foundation for their future success. You must understand the decisions you make can negatively impact your business and profits in the future, such as spending thousands to build their website and falling short on marketing.

What I provide for my clients is both the tools to get to their destination and also the education on how to get there. You have the choice of being able to build your business the proper way, and get on the fast track for success. Or you can get lost a few times, struggling find someone who can point you in the right direction.

So now you're ready to move towards your goals. Maybe you have an idea and want to figure out how to create success for it; or you have already built something and are looking to achieve your goals; or you know that you want to make more money, but are not sure how yet.

I have carefully created this entire system to help you, regardless of the product you are selling, or the service you are providing. In fact, this program takes you through the entire process of getting from where you are right now, how to set your destination and then how to use these strategies get to where you want to be.

My goal is to assist you on your journey to success and giving you access to the products, systems and my team to help you along the way. I am dedicated to assisting you to build your success. And I am honored that you are taking the time to read my book.

This book is available in different formats. Put this audio on in your car, on your computer, while you are working out, or where ever you are to keep up. No excuses, hold yourself accountable and push yourself to build your success. Know that you can achieve anything; you just have to put in the effort.

THE SEVEN PILLARS

PILLAR 1

CHAPTER 1

ARE YOU READY?

This might sound insane to you, but the number one thing holding you back from success is yourself. In February 2014, one of my millionaire mentors and I had dinner in a swanky midtown New York City restaurant. After the first bottle of the best wine I have ever had, he asked me, "What are your goals for this year?"

I went on talking for a few minutes, uninterrupted.

Then he followed up by asking, "Are you ready for the next level?"

After a few minutes talking, he repeated, "That is all nice, but are you ready?"

That stopped me in my tracks.

At this point, I had already generated tens of millions of dollars in revenue for my clients. I had the *Million Dollar Plan* formula years before, and I was only implementing for my clients. Not for my business.

Why would I make others millions in revenue, yet continue to work for an hourly rate?

I held myself back because I was scared. I feared for the unknown. I made poor life choices, such as spending $4,000 a month in rent or dating the wrong girl. I was easily distracted, and easily persuaded to venture in the wrong direction. Often times, the opposite direction of success and personal growth.

I was too interested in hanging out with the cool people, going out to trendy bars and traveling the world. My focus was on living a lifestyle that was not creating wealth. There was very little stability in my life and I was just getting by. In 2014, I was not ready for success. I had all the potential for greatness, but I was not ready. Something had to change in my life, I had to break out of my complacency and take a step back in order to take a giant leap forward.

RISK EVERYTHING

The first order of business was to create a big plan and immediately take massive action. I wrote up several new business ideas, attended events, and became active networking every opportunity I had. I created profiles on venture capital websites, and began reaching out to wealthy entrepreneurs for advice.

Needless to say, I went all in; I began purchasing every course I could find from every entrepreneur who taught how to build successful online brands. I needed to learn what makes the most successful entrepreneurs tick.

Through my research, I found an opportunity to build online training for entrepreneurs, write books and document my journey to success. I began investing in employees, software, hardware and everything I would need to create my online presence. Next came advertising to grow my presence.

I did not hold back at all. If I launched a program and it did not work, I quickly moved onto the next product launch. I spent no time wallowing in self-pity. It was go time, and there is no such thing as failure.

It truly takes undeniable dedication to reach your goals. I put the vacations on hold, started learning to say no to friends and focused my energy on my goals every day. I was constantly thinking bigger and learning from those who you would want to trade places with. Understanding this, I realized that I could no longer take on small projects from clients, realizing that my most valuable commodity I owned was my time. And with that, I needed to value my time over any other monetary value.

This allowed me to start setting aside my complacency and made me start moving every day like the building was on fire. It was then I also realized this is why you see so many rags to riches stories. These people who go from living on the street to driving Ferraris and living in mansions. They move like they are going to go hungry if they don't achieve their success. Because many of the homeless to millionaire stories begin with going hungry.

Up until this time in life, I always had a safety net with my family. But I cut the cord and didn't look back. It was time for me to fly or die, so I jumped.

CHANGED MY LIFE

The change in my life has been interesting to say the least. I no longer stare at the clock, waiting or just merely clocking hours in life. I no longer focus on the hours that I work, nor care about the things in life that do not matter.

It is crazy to think that you can train your mind and condition yourself for greatness. For instance, I have trained myself to produce the same amount of work in a day that used to take a week. I have been inspired by my mentors and historical greats like Muhammad Ali, who I had the honor of meeting in real life.

My life has turned into the following process: learn, build, test, analyze, pivot, test, analyze, build, test, analyze, build, test and eventually scale!

What does that mean? Building a successful business all breaks down to testing new ideas, analyzing the results and then retesting to find what is working. And there are entrepreneurs like me who publish our findings online through training, so others can follow in our footsteps to create their success.

This has become my new life, as I am building an empire through my 30s, and perhaps you are reading this book several years into the future, while I am relaxing on my yacht in my 40s. Or perhaps I fall flat on my face, and I am working my tail off into my 40s to build back up to success. I am ready for any challenge life throws at me, and I meet every challenge with a positive attitude and an open mind.

But regardless of where I am in the world, and what is going on with my life, it is now time to focus on you and your success.

A NEW DAY

The days when a single median household income can support a family are gone. And those days may never return. Costs for everything are going up, and the desire to purchase more expensive gadgets, cars and other luxury items is on the rise.

Unfortunately, our incomes are not rising to meet those desires for bigger purchases. This trend can be seen worldwide, through the world debt crisis and media. You cannot turn on the TV today without seeing advertisements for products, and the flashiness of those product placements on celebrities.

We want more and we want it faster. This is driving people online to create businesses, and at the same time, creating more consumers for products. The end goal for new entrepreneurs and consumers is to use the Internet to achieve their objectives faster and easier.

As an entrepreneur, your focus should be to understand who your target demographic is, what they want, what their interests are, and be able to convince them to buy your product within one minute of them visiting your website. Sounds easy enough, right?

Engaging your target audience is a science and not an overnight accomplishment. Engagement and sales begin with research. Understanding your target demographic and what they want is difficult; but as a business owner, you will need to learn how to get inside your audience's mind.

Mentioning this, reminds me of the not quite Oscar-worthy movie featuring Mel Gibson called "What Women Want." Gibson plays a chauvinistic ad executive who gains the ability to hear what women are really thinking.

This allows him to get inside women's minds to understand what they truly want, both in their personal lives and for the product in his ad campaign. Thus, Gibson's character was able to create a successful ad campaign that identified with his target audience.

Unfortunately, real life does not work like the movies. But the concept is similar; you will need to commit yourself to understanding your target audience, in order to create an online presence that will attract customers.

If you do not like spending time in a restaurant, perhaps you shouldn't open one. If you know nothing about women's fashion, don't try and create an online store selling women's clothes.

Put yourself in the mind of your target audience and try to view your product through their eyes. Understand their interests outside your business, so you will be able to know how to market to them.

WHERE TO START?

Businesses all begin at different starting points. I have worked with clients who started their business because they want to make more money. Some of my clients wanted to be their own boss, while others began their companies accidentally by falling into something they love to do. Regardless of your starting point, you have the desire to sell products or services to customers.

There are so many options on how to get your business started: there are do-it-yourself website builders, online courses to start a business, books, online portals to hire people, and so many blogs to read.

There is a good chance this book is not your first attempt at starting your business. Many of my new clients have previously worked with other business development experts and web developers or tried to get started on their own.

In fact, I really enjoy working with new clients after they attend seminars because they're fired up, excited and are willing to invest in their business. Ironically, many of these seminars feature content on how to build a business, but yet many attendees remain confused on where to start.

Why is this?

Many of these seminars and events are narrowly focused and do not explain the big picture. Please note, not every event is like this. However, many entrepreneurs created their success with a specific formula, which does not apply to every business model.

Unfortunately, these seminars do not take into account the student's background, business or knowledge level. All too often, these seminars are narrowly focused on one aspect of business, like social media marketing for example. Many of the seminars miss the mark on business planning, market research and identifying opportunity. Entrepreneurs are so ready to take their product to market; however, they have not researched to understand their opportunity. Is this the right product? Is this the right demographic?

For example, several start-up formulas take a heavy online approach using video marketing. Several of my clients are not comfortable with creating videos or audio for their business. On the other hand, sometimes it is good to get out of your comfort zone and see what works for your business. It is safe to say that every new entrepreneur needs guidance along the way from someone who has been there before.

There are thousands of different ways to connect with your target audience. You have to find what works for you and learn how to attract your potential customers to your offers. But we are getting too far ahead of ourselves. We first must start with a business plan. Your business plan is the most important piece of your company, and it is never too late to revisit your plan.

YOUR PLAN

Did you already write a business plan? That is great! Don't skip this section though. I promise that every business owner will need to review this, even if you feel that your plan is perfect as-is.

The first place to start with your business plan is with your customers. Yes, you read that right. From day 1, just focus on your customers. For years I didn't understand this. I didn't see the human element to sales nor did I understand the psychology of why people buy. But let's face it, I am just an average student after all.

Everyone wants something and your goal is to provide people with what they want. Explaining why they want this and how this thing you are selling will give them pleasure. Let's face it — marketing is just about the pain and pleasure.

If you can take away one item from this book, make sure it is learning who your target audience is and how to solve a problem in their lives. Start by understanding your audience and what frustrates them.

Is there something keeping them up at night or causing pain? Is it emotional or physical? If you solve their problems, you will create success in your life. Yes, success really is that easy. Solve your customer's problems, and you will have a winning product or service.

You should also pay closer attention to infomercials on TV. It's silly to say, but the marketing people behind many of those products have really honed this skill. And in many cases, the skill of visually expressing pain and pleasure is — at times — entertaining.

While writing your business plan, keep those infomercials in mind, in addition to your audience and their frustrations. It's time to start writing.

- What is the objective of your business?
- Who is your target audience?
- What are their frustrations?
- Why do they need to buy your product?
- How does your product make your customer's life better?
- What makes your product better than your competitor's product?
- How can you beat your competitor in the marketplace?

As you begin filling in the blanks, your product's marketing plan will reveal itself.

FOR THE PEOPLE

One of the top complaints from business owners is low engagement on their social media accounts. "How do I get more comments, likes, shares, follows and fans?"

All too often the business owner will jump to blame Facebook for changing their systems or Twitter for being a horrible place for conversations. But this is not the real problem.

The problem is much bigger than likes on social media. Social media is only illuminating the bigger issue in the business, not connecting with your customers. If you are unable to connect with your audience, they may not ever purchase from you. If they make a purchase and your customer care is terrible, there is a good chance they will not purchase again.

It is crazy that my dry cleaner is better at customer care, follow-up, email marketing and social media than most businesses. It is dry cleaning; there is nothing exciting about it!

But for some reason, the company invested effort into creating a great experience. Some of that is automated, which we will get into in detail in future chapters, but some aspects of their customer care began in the beginning.

That is where you need to start with your business. Without your people, you will not have a business. Your people include your customers, potential customers and employees. Put their interests above yours and the bottom line, and you will improve your probability for sustainable success.

DO NOT DABBLE

Commit yourself 100% to your business and do not let anyone distract or move you from your path to success. It is crazy how we can read a book or watch a video from our mentor, and rethink our plan. Don't let it happen. You can lose weeks or months by changing your plan.

See your plan through to completion, and if it doesn't work, feel free to backtrack and retest that idea that you had. Keep a journal of notes on your ideas and go back to test ideas that were not part of your original plan.

Stay focused and don't listen to the naysayers. The only people you should take advice from are those who you look up to, and you would happily trade places with them. There are so many people online today who are giving horrible advice and leading entrepreneurs in the wrong direction.

Although the Internet gives everyone the ability to have a voice, when it comes to your business, stay focused and do not let others lead you astray. If someone gives you advice, ask them to see some validation on why you should take their advice. Think about your business as your baby, you wouldn't trust the health and well-being of your baby to anyone with an Internet connection, would you? Be careful of who you trust online and always ask questions.

Remember, your time is your most valuable commodity and you must remove your time from the equation in order to create wealth. You cannot get rich while working at an hourly rate.

THE SEVEN PILLARS

PILLAR 2

CHAPTER 2

WHAT IS HOLDING
YOU BACK?

I s your fear holding you back? Are you scared of failure? Fearful you will not have the money to pay your bills this month or scared that you don't know how to create success?

There are so many fears that can hold us back from success, but know that fears are not real. Eviction, on the other hand, is real. I know because I have been asked to leave when I previously couldn't pay rent. But the fear of not being able to pay rent is not real.

Our fears can often paralyze us and hold us back from creating success. We spend more time worrying about our fears and the unknown that we lose time thinking about creating wealth. Train your mind to remove the fears and replace the fears in your mind with positive thoughts of success.

When I start thinking about success, I imagine creating solutions and thinking of ways how I can help people. What keeps you awake at night? Paying your bills on time? Thinking about how you will afford that next big purchase? Worried about money in general?

Thinking of ways to help people keeps me awake at night. Sure, the name of this book is *Million Dollar Plan*, but it is not all about money to me. Money is only a tool to help us get to where we want to be. And I want to help more people change their lives for the better. I want to help entrepreneurs build successful businesses, hire more staff, pay their staff well, and encourage others to give to those who are less fortunate than us. Without money, none of that dream is possible.

YOUR BIGGEST HURDLE

The number one killer of businesses is procrastination. Looking back over the last 20 years, it seems that life is getting more interesting and there are distractions around every corner. Or perhaps my perceptions are my reality.

Let's take cell phones for example. I have been working since I was 14 years old, and when I wasn't in school, I was expected to work 40-hour weeks. From my labors, I was able to afford a cell phone at the young age of 15. Today that doesn't seem all too exciting, but trust me, in 1998 that was a big deal!

I remember it today, my Nokia cell phone, so exciting. And this was the new model where you could change the faceplate of the phone to one of the cool designs. It was the beginning of self-expression in your technology, exciting times!

This phone came with one game installed — snake. The objective of the game was to click the buttons up, down, left and right to guide a line around the screen to pick up dots. Each time the line touched a dot, the line became longer. And you would lose by touching the line on itself, or by traveling outside the screen area.

Wow, this game is really boring to think about today, but I must have put in 100 hours on that game. My first couple jobs were hands on, and I did not have much downtime at all. But I can pinpoint my professional procrastination back to the job I took in 2001 at a computer store. I was the only sales person on the floor, and there was a tech in the back, working on cleaning out viruses from customer's machines.

There were some days at the store when I didn't see a customer all day. We played a movie in the store, but the owners never changed it, which was probably to keep me focused on selling, even though no one ever came in. I became a pro solitaire player, hearts and minesweeper. But my biggest distraction came from my Nokia phone. I would sit in the bathroom for hours and play snake on my phone. I didn't want to do anything else but play that game.

Comparing my addiction to technology then to the distractions that exist today is no comparison. The games today are 100 times better, more addicting and more entertaining. Am I 100 times more addicted? No. Did I grow up to become an adult? Maybe. Perhaps I matured a little bit, but not that much.

Today my biggest distractions are from my clients, advertising, emails and social media. Sure, I still have video games, movies and TV to keep me distracted, but it is not that hard to set a schedule and stick to it! Just a touch of willpower and you can be successful with time management.

I am distracted because I am connected. My emails pop up, and I cannot stand having that little notification of unread anything on my phone or computer, so I have to clear that out. While doing so, I typically come across something from a client that needs my attention. This was one of the biggest issues when I was just getting started with my business, but now I have the ability to delegate these tasks. But the Catch-22 is how do you grow to hire people and delegate if you are unable to be productive?

You just have to push through or it will take years to accomplish your goals. Yes, procrastination comes in many different shapes and sizes, disguised as a friend inviting you out for a drink, or even as a celebration of your success.

I wouldn't be surprised if procrastination is one of the biggest factors to businesses failing. Owners can misplace advertising budgets, hire the wrong people or make fatal mistakes with their businesses. But I believe that all mistakes can be resolved. It just takes the willingness to make a difference and taking massive action.

TAKING MASSIVE ACTION

First, what is massive action?

If you just take action, you can achieve a six-figure business in the first year, which is not very hard to do if you commit yourself to success. However, massive action is the act of taking your goals and multiplying by 10. Then, take the goal and build a new plan to reach for higher success. I encourage every client I work with to think bigger.

If you have a plan for opening one store this year, let's figure out how to open 10 stores instead. If you want to become a best-selling author this year, how do we launch 10 new books to the best seller list?

Sometimes our goals are far beyond our reach, but if we set our goals too low, we will not take massive action to reach our goals.

My favorite stories are about desperation and starting from nothing because stories are motivational and uplifting. A few entrepreneurs have gone from homeless to millionaire in just a few years. How is that possible? They move like the building is on fire!

There are so many new businesses starting every day, and many of these entrepreneurs have some startup capital to get started. Yet, many of these middle class entrepreneurs get beat out by people starting with nothing. Perhaps I like these stories because I can relate. I started with nothing. Even though I never thought of myself as being homeless, it's only because I have always had someone to lean on for support.

The point here is it doesn't matter where you are starting, or how much money you are starting with. You only need the desire to do whatever it takes to be successful, and you need to work like you are desperate and you hit rock bottom. The next problem that you will run into is complacency, and this will be another tough hurdle in your business. Again, you will need to push through and always remind yourself why you started this business and what you are working towards.

GOALS

Complacency can be overcome by writing down your goals — daily, weekly, monthly and yearly. Yes, I have goals for each segment of time, and then I track these goals through to completion or failure.

Without goals, it is easy to fall into contentment and be fine with your current situation. I've experienced this before, and many of my friends and family operate in a constant state of complacency, which is perfectly fine.

But you might wake up one day, like I did, and say "my biggest fear is mediocrity." I define mediocre as, "not improving myself or my situation day to day, week to week, month to month and year to year."

Growing up, I was always told that "you can be anything you want to be." And I think that went in one ear and out the other, like many other things my parents told me when I was a kid. However, I believe that something stuck in my subconscious mind — I can accomplish anything I set my mind to. And no, I did not believe this coming out of college or even in my early career. After taking a job in New York City and seeing how the top 1 percent lived, I started to understand what they meant.

I set goals for myself — smaller daily goals, all the way up to mega goals that I have not achieved yet (this book becoming a best seller is one of them). But as I am writing these words, obviously the book is not a best seller. What I know is that it will become a best-selling book, regardless because I refuse to let this book fail. You know how sometimes you say things out loud, but you really don't believe your own words?

That doesn't happen with me. What I say CAN and WILL happen.

Once you fully embrace this mindset and set your goals high, watch out world! Here comes ___(fill in your name here)___!

If you want something, put together a plan to achieve it. Start your plan at the goal and work backwards with small tasks to reach the end goal. Fill in the parts you don't know with advice from people who have accomplished those tasks before.

This is really not difficult and works with just about any goal that you can set for yourself. The number one thing is to not spread yourself too thin, or to bite off more than you can chew. Pick one goal and create a path to achieve it. If the path or goal changes a bit, that is fine. Just don't lose sight of why you started and never quit.

And always take massive action.

IT IS GO TIME

Some of you might be thinking now "my goal is to become the wealthiest person on the planet, revolutionize every industry and become a business tycoon. Matt's book said that I can accomplish anything I set my mind to. So it is going to happen."

However, you need to stay inside your genius zone as you are crafting your idea. That is not to say you cannot plan for your time in the equation to study your industry more in-depth as you become the top producer.

In 2003, I had the idea that could revolutionize the way we drive our cars. I was so set on my dream and ideas that I started contacting people in the automobile industry to figure out how to make this dream reality. I was even looking at moving out west where I could have property to build my test facility.

Yes, my idea was far outside my wheelhouse, so far outside that it was on a different planet. There wasn't a single aspect of this plan that I knew anything about, and I would have to spend years of my life devoted solely to creating my solution for better automobile travel. Did I completely give up on my dreams? Did I sell myself short? Did I tell myself that I wasn't good enough?

No. I created a more realistic plan and perhaps one day my dream still will happen. Or perhaps my dream will be proven to be a crazy idea that doesn't work. Regardless, now I have enough money to test my ideas to try and make them happen. Create your plan around your ideas that you can execute to build wealth, then leverage your wealth to invest into yourself and solving the world's problems.

My inspiration is Elon Musk, an entrepreneur who started a software company, Zip2, in 1995 that sold for $307 million four years later. Musk then rolled his earnings into a new company that became PayPal. A few years later, Musk sold PayPal to eBay and walked away with $165 million, which then he invested into projects like SpaceX, Tesla Motors and Hyperloop. Here is a guy who started in software and now is planning manned missions to Mars.

If Musk took his father's $28,000 investment to start up Zip2, and invested it into his dream of private manned missions to Mars, he would have wasted every penny. However, he took a small investment and became a millionaire in a few years, then reinvested into making his other worldly dreams a reality. Twenty years after borrowing money from his father, Musk is revolutionizing industries and inspiring entrepreneurs around the world.

If your idea is to travel to distant galaxies, or create a new app in iTunes, regardless of how big or how small, your dreams and ideas are yours. Don't let anyone take those away from you. However, create realistic plans to achieve your goals by creating wealth and leveraging your influence to make your dreams happen.

YOUR MILLION DOLLAR IDEA

I cannot give you your million-dollar idea. What I can do is encourage you to dig deeper. Think bigger and reach beyond the limits that you place on yourself.

One of the best places to start is to look at your competition. In many cases, your competition has been in business for years longer than you have, and they have spent their own money testing what is and isn't working. With that theory in mind, you can assume the advertising and presence your competitors have is what is working today.

Or perhaps your competition is going about business all wrong, and your opportunity is in filling the void they are not filling with their products and services. That is up for you to decide. And yes, you would be correct if you said to yourself, "this sounds like a guessing game." Because that is exactly what this is — guessing.

As you become more seasoned in business, your guessing might become better and perhaps you become a great guesser. I consider myself a seasoned guesser, meaning I can look at any part of a company's online presence and guess how I would make it better. Then I can execute that plan faster than most others, because I have already tested the idea in the past.

Start by learning how to get your prospective clients and customers to pay attention to your message. Although it is not easy, this is the time to leverage a mentor or someone who knows what to look for in this situation. And yes, I try my best to respond to every email that I receive with the best advice I can give.

As you are drafting your million-dollar plan, keep in mind a basic outline for startup capital, resources and your time. Estimate how much money it will take to get your plan moving, what resources you will need, and start creating timelines to achieve your goals. Also keep in mind that money is easy to come by, if you have the right plan.

Again, if you get stuck at any point in your planning process or if you get the plan on paper and you are not confident, find someone who can help you create your breakthrough in your planning. If you cannot find anyone to help you, email me and I will help you the best I can.

Think big, set your goals high, create a timeline and hold yourself accountable. Take massive action and get started on your plan today!

KNOW YOUR CUSTOMERS

Listen to your customers, if you do not already have customers, then you should survey your friends and family. Leverage every source of information you can, create your marketing research and define your market opportunity.

There are so many ways to approach your venture and identifying your opportunities. Some say to look for gaps in the marketplace, while others suggest that a great place to start researching is where your future competitors are failing. You will find the best brainstorming environment that works for you.

For me, I have had every big idea while I am in the shower. This is not a lie. I spend my time in thought exercises and even have found myself copywriting while in the shower. Perhaps that is why someone created a tape recorder for the shower years back. Some people sing, I create million-dollar business plans.

Once you have the idea, start surveying your potential customers and getting an understanding of their frustrations and how you can solve their frustrations with your product or service. Understand why people buy similar products, out of necessity or as an impulse. Break down the buying habits, and start spending your time people watching in stores. There is much to learn from people in shopping malls, and I learned this from years of being dragged to malls against my will.

I am the other type of buyer, one who is in and out. I have a need, and this product solves my need and I would like to purchase. Often I will do a quick price compare, leveraging the Internet to see if I can find the product cheaper online. Then I take into consideration how quickly I need the item, and I make my decision. If I am your target demographic, take this information into consideration as you are building your marketing plan.

Understand who your customers are, and what frustrates them. Create solutions and show the value of your product. Do not be afraid to price your product high to be the premium product on the market, or do not be afraid to explore the other end of the spectrum and beat your competitors on price. Regardless, understand why people buy and use your product to fill a gap in their lives. If you accomplish this, you will have a winning product and business.

THE SEVEN PILLARS

PILLAR 3

CHAPTER 3

STANDING OUT

While creating your *Million Dollar Plan*, start thinking about how you can stand out of the crowd. If your product or service is plain, then you will need to stand out in other ways. Create a loud brand and make noise in your industry. Become a disrupter, either with your innovation or with your marketing. But keep in mind, the more ordinary your business is, the more money for advertising it will take to stand out.

The more noise and disruption that you can make, the more people will share your product with their friends and family on social media. All too often my clients ask me why their messages are not getting likes and shares on social media. It is primarily because the message is simple and straightforward. Let your creativity flourish and be willing to do something different.

The company that comes to mind is Dollar Shave Club. This company set out to shake up the razorblade industry by offering decent razors at a cheaper price. Then the company went forward to create a goofy video that went viral on social media. In fact, I tried to buy razors from this company and they were so much on back order that I was unable to purchase an item from them.

You are saying to yourself, "so Matt, just make my video go viral and I will make a million dollars." Sorry, it doesn't work like that. No one can guarantee viral activity on your media, although I have had videos go viral in the past. But it is definitely not every video that goes viral. The key here is to keep working until something catches on like wildfire.

Although razors are boring, somehow the company found a way to stand out and get massive attention. Now their cost for marketing is much less than having to force their advertising into the world. What do I mean by that? Keep in mind, any company can sell millions in products, but it might cost you millions to sell millions. The secret here is to find a voice and stand out where you will not need a hefty ad budget to get noticed.

Leverage the latest technology and find new ways to connect with your audience. This all begins with your marketing plan as you come up with big ideas to reach millions of eyeballs. You'll then create an offer or marketing message that will get those people to take action. Research your competition and brainstorm ideas. Don't be afraid to get creative.

YOUR COMPETITION

Research your competition, study them, buy their products, breakdown their processes and find out what makes them tick. And if you are thinking to yourself that you do not have any competition, let me stop you right there. You do have some form of competition, look harder for them.

Break down your competitors into three different groups: 1) the top producers 2) your peers and 3) those who are not executing very well.

The top producers are those who you would happily trade places with. Perhaps their product is the "talk of the town" or they just seem to be everywhere. Break down how they became a top producer and find ways to "hack" their methods to follow their path to success.

You can learn from your peers, who are on the same level as you. Do not put yourself on a higher level than them, or think you are above them. Even if you think you are better than they are, you can still learn something to capture more customers. Also, keep in mind your peers might one day become a top producer.

Lastly in your marketplace are those who are lost and are trying to compete with you, but you can't help and think they are one day away from going out of business. Don't let these people in your space fool you. Instead keep an eye on them. Someone like me can come through and invest in a company or build resources to create a successful online brand and take over your place in the market. I have seen this happen before!

The moral of this story is to keep an eye on everyone in your marketplace, regardless of where they are in the process of marketing and their online presence. Also know that likes on Facebook are no indication of how well a company is performing in sales. Likes do not pay the bills!

Try to go down to your local food store and buy anything in the store with your likes on Facebook. I have tried, it definitely does not work! It does not matter how many followers you have on social media; it is very hard to post a message and then cash in that message for a bite to eat. Always remember to stay focused on the real goals and every post on social media is just one more touch with your potential buyer before they make a purchase.

Immerse yourself in your industry and do anything you can to connect with every influencer and network with those who can help take your business to the next level. Invest your time and money in trade shows, events, books and any other education that can give you a leg up on your competition. Becoming a top producer takes pulling out all the stops and giving it everything you got.

YOUR CUSTOMERS

Learn from your customers and find out what makes them tick. Understand their frustrations, their fears and what keeps them up at night. If you are able to solve their problems, you will reach your goals. How do you learn all this information? Interview your customers or your potential customers if you do not have any yet.

You can accomplish this by making surveys, or just the old-fashioned way of picking up the phone to follow-up with your customers. Trust me, a majority of your customers will appreciate the human touch and the sound of a caring voice. Often, we hide behind technology but take the effort to reach beyond it to make your customers feel special. Sure technology can do this at times for us, and with email automation, this can be simple. But don't hide behind your technology all the time.

As you are building your business, think of ways you can go above and beyond for your customers. This also comes back to researching your competitors, finding ways to help your customers feel better doing business with you, and they will become repeat customers. Here is the hierarchy of my business: customers, employees, and then myself. Always put your customers first in your business and your employees second.

Create raving fans through understanding what your customers want and then provide that for them. All too often my clients can become disconnected from their customers, and running the business can be quite overwhelming. I've worked with massive companies over the years, and I can honestly say that customer service is not top of mind for many CEOs. Am I saying that every CEO should micromanage their customer service? No. But every CEO should have a report or pulse on what their customers are thinking.

ONLINE REPUTATION

Your online reputation might not make you a million dollars a year, but it could cost you a million per year. Keep that in mind as you are building your company. One of my previous clients started their business around the turn of the millennium, and for years the owner would say "as long as the credit cards keep running, what do I care what a few wackos say in some forum?" Needless to say, he should have cared more.

This client ended up being penalized from Facebook, Google and other marketing sources because of this poor reputation, and had to begin a massive campaign to thwart the negative reputation online to salvage advertising relationships to stay in business. One way or another, negative actions or comments can catch up with you. Personally, I try my hardest to overcome negative comments from the beginning, and I never argue with my customers. If I did not meet your expectations, tell me what I have to do to make it right.

Take a similar approach for your business and do whatever you can to make it right. Perhaps the customer will never buy from you again, and perhaps you were right and the customer was wrong. Regardless of the circumstances, rise above the pettiness and learn how you can make it right for the next customer. Take your company's reputation seriously, and keep a pulse on what your customers are saying about your products and services.

In the past few years, Google has created an awesome free tool called Google Alerts. With this simple application, you can set up a system to track keywords and trends that are posted to Google in real time. Meaning, if you want to track mentions about your business online, you can set up an alert to send you an email or notify you when something has been written about your business. This is just another way that Google is providing free tools to make our business easier to run and manage our online reputations by leveraging technology.

SOLVING A PROBLEM

As you are creating your product or service, brainstorm what people are complaining about and start watching trends. Open your eyes and become aware of the problems that are facing people in their everyday lives. Ultimately, this activity of brainstorming has created some of the most successful businesses over the last 20 years. Or at the very least, entrepreneurs have leveraged technology and frustrations to create amazing products and services that make our lives easier.

There are some amazing websites online that you can leverage to keep your pulse on trends and new businesses launching. For example, I follow tech blogs and other investment websites that report on the newest technology coming out, and I use these publications to brainstorm the projects that I am working on. Submerse yourself in innovation and the new trends. Then you will eventually find yourself becoming innovative and trend setting.

You do not have to look far to see the trend setters and the innovation today that is powering our world that we live in. And if you think that everything worth inventing has already been invented, you are dead wrong. Entrepreneurs will continue being innovative and changing the landscape of the marketplace as long as there are people still alive on this planet. When we venture off to colonize other worlds, it will be entrepreneurs like Elon Musk who take us there and perhaps entrepreneurs like you who begin changing the new world that has not been colonized yet.

It truly is an exciting time to be alive and as entrepreneurs, we can make our business improving the lives of others. Currently there are more than three billion people with the Internet, and entrepreneurs like Mark Zuckerberg are trying to expand it to reach those who are not already connected. That means, that sometime in the future, there could be double or triple that amount of people who can be reached through Facebook marketing.

Think about this - if you are able to create a product that improves people's lives, you could potentially reach over one billion people today on Facebook alone. And in the future, you could reach more as Facebook grows over the next 10 years. Similar to Facebook, Google has also a reach of over one billion people and continues to grow. If you could earn just $1 from those people, you would be one of the top wealthiest entrepreneurs in the world.

Is earning $1 per person your business plan? Probably not. But it is interesting to think about how far technology has come in the last 10 years, or even think back to starting a business before the Internet. Our parents and grandparents who started businesses were limited to their neighbors and by their media coverage. Sure, there have been forms of advertising since the 1800s, but the ability to launch a business and reach a million people within a single day is insanity.

For example: I shot a video October 13, 2010 and uploaded to YouTube. Five hours later, that video had over one million views and was on the front page of Yahoo and YouTube 10 hours later. After that, I had calls from CNN, ABC, NBC, FOX and just about every other network asking to use my video. I reached over 2 million people on my YouTube channel alone and tens of millions through the television with my video of balloons over NYC. Is that a business? No. But I shot a quick video of balloons to prove to my friends that the "UFO Sighting" over NYC was just balloons, and then it ended up going viral. I made a few thousand dollars from ads though.

Is creating wacky viral content solving a problem? No. But creating the next system that helps circulate news faster could be the next big thing. Or perhaps a new way to learn about viral content. It is exciting to think about what is possible, and what could be the next big thing. You could be its founder. You may also find a way to cure sicknesses, or how to travel to the further planet in our galaxy. Two problems to solve are pollution and energy. Someone should get started on the pollution, while another begins work on cancer and other sicknesses that are killing millions of people each year.

Regardless of the path you take, be sure that you are interested in your business and you feel that you could work on your business for the rest of your life. If there is even a slight chance that you will hate the new company you are starting, take a step back and evaluate again why you are starting your business. To me, I love helping people, and the more entrepreneurs that I can help, the more people who are less fortunate that I can help. That is why I donate a percentage of every dollar made from my online training programs to charity. And I encourage my clients to do the same. With more of us giving back, and being thoughtful to helping others, perhaps we can truly make a difference in the world to improve other's lives for the better.

PAIN & PLEASURE

Hopefully some of you are working on solving all the world's problems! But for those of you who are not curing cancer, we will need to talk about advertising a bit. Let's face it, if your business is curing cancer, then you will have no need for understanding how to advertise. However, for those of us who will not have the benefit of massive media exposure, we will need to learn how to create our own message, write our own story and leave an impression with our potential customers.

Successful advertising boils down to the pain and the pleasure. Again, think back to those cheesy infomercials on TV, and in your best announcer voice say: "Are you tired of this" as the black and white video plays of some actor over-acting on something that is painful. Back to the announcer voice: "Introducing, the all new gadget! This will change your life forever!" And the video goes to color, and the product is on screen making the actor's life so much easier. That is the pain and pleasure.

Without your product, the person's life will be just miserable. But their life becomes easier and better by purchasing the item. Does every ad need to follow this template? No. But a majority of advertising does follow the pain and pleasure template for attracting customers. At some point in your marketing, test out different ads and try to follow this template to see how you can showcase the benefits of your product through solving the frustrations of your customers.

This is perhaps the number one thing that could be holding your business back from creating your game-changer ad campaign. Honestly, you only need one great ad or slogan to change your life and your business forever! Just turn on the TV and watch for the commercials, and I guarantee you that there will be at least one commercial that has been using the same slogan for more than a year. Some companies are still using the same ads, rotated in years later.

All too often, I see new clients who complain about traffic sources or advertising to say, "I tested that and it does not work." I do not believe these statements one bit. The ad platform will work, with the correct ad and the right landing page and the right message. If you are unable to write compelling messages, learn how to write better sales copy. Hire someone to work with you, and train you on how to write better text and create better advertising. A poor performing ad campaign is usually an indication that something is wrong with your targeting, or perhaps your understanding of the market opportunity and your customer's frustrations. Take a deeper look beyond saying, "It just didn't work."

MARKET OPPORTUNITY

Before we get too ahead of ourselves, let's go through the brainstorming process for finding your market opportunity and better understanding the target demographics. Definitely leverage the free tools that are online through Google and Facebook to find your target audience size. Think about Google as the tool that helps you reach customers who are looking for something, and Facebook as the device that will help you find customers based upon their interests.

For example, if your business is fixing iPhones after someone drops theirs, you would use Google to target "iPhone screen replacement" or other keywords that people would type into Google. And Google has a free keyword tool that will help you break down the location and volume that is being searched, trends in when the volume has spiked and the competition for that keyword. Google also provides alternate keywords to consider and the estimated cost per click to put your offer in front of the potential customer who dropped their phone recently.

However, Facebook would not be the best place to advertise this company, as it is harder to target people who dropped their phone recently and need repairs. It's not to say that marketing on Facebook would not work for this business. It just shows how this company could leverage Google better for on-demand services like phone repair.

On the other hand, a new author selling a book might find Facebook to be more helpful. The author could target by interests and knowing what future readers are interested in would help guide you towards your potential future sales. Facebook gathers information about its users and aggregates that content through the Facebook Ads platform to allow advertisers to target users based upon their interests, demographics and other trends that have been compiled into the system generated from your activity on the social network site.

Sharing a bit of my marketing strategy for this book, I will be leveraging Facebook mostly to target my ads to people who have bought business books from my competitors. Or perhaps target my competitors who have not written books yet. With that targeting strategy through Facebook, I am able to place my ads in front of my competitor's audience with the hopes that if the customer is interested in my competitor's message, perhaps they might be interested in my book and offers. In future chapters we will dive deeper into marketing strategies, and when is the best time to use Facebook and Google.

These are not the only forms of advertising. There are other methods such as retargeting and other forms of interest-based display ads on Google. However, the meaning of mentioning this was not to go in-depth with an advertising strategy, rather to help you understand where the opportunity for reaching your target audience might exist and some of the tools that are available today to help you research, plan and execute an advertising campaign.

EDUCATE

Entrepreneurship is on the rise and will continue to expand to the furthest reaches of the planet. If you are starting up a new industry today, you could potentially have new competitors next month. All this is thanks to the ability to launch new websites and advertise new products and services faster than ever before. How do you continue to compete in the marketplace?

The answer is education. Educate your customers and potential customers about the benefits of your product or service. You can help them understand the benefits of purchasing from you through text, video and imagery. Leverage the blog on your website, and if you do not have a blog, get one started. Use your posts to educate your potential customers, and also reach those customers through your social media profiles and advertising. The better you can educate your prospects, the more likely you can be to earn them as a customer.

Create a strong brand and online presence, educate your customer and engage your customer. Just as I am writing this, I posted a funny video to my Facebook page. Does that video educate? Not really. Then how is a funny video helping? I posted the video to my Facebook fan page to get my followers to think about viral content for their website. So in essence, I am entertaining and educating at the same time in what other people are doing to grow their audiences through social media.

The only way to keep your product and services at the forefront of your customers and potential customers is by posting regularly and staying consistent with your emailing messaging as well. Consistency is important through social media, and then you can follow up with advertising to reinforce your offers and encourage prospective clients to buy right from your social media pages.

Also, you can use retargeting to capture the visitor's information and start advertising your offers through Facebook and Google. Facebook will track the user as they visited your website. Your ad campaigns can start within Facebook Ads as a follow-up to that education through your blog. And likewise on Google, your ads can follow through other websites that support Google ads throughout the Internet.

If you want to learn more about setting up advertising, I recommend that you join ScaleUP Academy, the online training program to teach you how to create a successful advertising campaign. ScaleUP Academy has the up-to-date marketing strategies that are working today, and you can follow along as we show you how to set up successful ad campaigns that drive results.

THE SEVEN PILLARS

PILLAR 4

CHAPTER 4

YOUR VOICE

The images that you use — your logo, the words posted to your social media, the emails that you send — all paints your brand identity and creates your voice. Often, new business owners will trust this voice to a graphic designer and, at times, the budget for hiring a branding consultant can hold back businesses from making a good impression. This leaves new companies handcuffed to poor graphic representations of their businesses and possibly conveying the wrong message to the marketplace.

You can only make a first impression once, but rebranding is an option. For some, rebranding can be expensive, so I definitely recommend saving money and putting effort into getting your brand identity right the first time. Luckily there are tools that you can leverage to create a brand image without breaking the bank.

If you feel that your brand is not being represented very well by your graphics or what you have already put into the world, it is OK. We have all made mistakes and even branding experts like myself had created a brand and voice, then have pivoted over the years to find our true calling.

Using my brand as an example, I have been all over the place as I work to find my purpose in the marketplace. My brand started with creating Elite Gurus, an online community of the top experts to help startups with web development and marketing. After gathering feedback from members and readers, I decided to take that brand over to create the ScaleUP brand that I use today. I own ScaleUP Consulting, ScaleUP Academy, ScaleUP 360 and ScaleUP Media, all sites that have their own purpose, products and messages under the ScaleUP umbrella.

During the time period of three years, I was working on a variety of different products and services, trying to find the best solutions that I can provide to the marketplace, and falling short on several occasions. However, I was able to continuously pivot on failures and reuse most of my content on the next solution that I launch for my members.

In the end, ScaleUP Academy formed as the home of all my training that I have created, including the Million Dollar Plan training guide. ScaleUP Media is the home of documenting this book launch and other book launches that I have managed, where future authors can learn how to write and launch a best-selling book. I offer my consulting services at ScaleUP Consulting. However, that is currently being rebranded towards becoming a certified consultant of my programs, serving both the community of consultants who follow the training and entrepreneurs who need to hire a consultant through our community.

It has taken years for me to find my voice, and at times my communities have sat dormant, waiting for the right time and plan to go forward. Rebranding and pivoting is an important part of being an entrepreneur and taking massive action, so do not get discouraged if you come to the conclusion that you need to pivot for your business. There are times that a step back is necessary to take a step forward into our greatness.

YOUR COMPANY NAME

This book is not going to name your company for you, but you can follow along through the steps that I have used to name several companies over the years. Naming a company comes down to four questions:

1) Branding yourself or building a business?
2) Is your company expanding beyond your city?
3) Include your product or service in the name?
4) Can you get that name as a domain?

Let's start with branding yourself or building a business, which should be super easy for you to answer. If you are planning on creating a public figure, or making yourself into a celebrity of sorts or author or musician, then consider using your name. Otherwise, let's go to the drawing board for coming up with a company name.

Keep in mind, the holy grail of branding a new company is to make your company name work as a verb, and even more challenging, making your brand a household name. An example is Google, as people refer to using a search engine to "Google it." Because of this and many other reasons, Google owns roughly 65% of the U.S. search engine market share in 2016. And you can imagine how difficult it is for a company like Bing to compete with a verb as a colossal giant in the search engine space. Will your company name become a household name? It is possible, not probable though.

For argument's sake, let's say your brand is not going to become a household name, but do you have plans in the future to expand beyond your city or region? I have run into this problem with clients in the past where the company is branded as the city, state or region where the company started, and then is looking to expand beyond that area. It is important to have an idea of expansion in your business plan at the beginning and plan accordingly. If you start locally and need to rebrand for growth, that is great and means you are taking massive action. Congratulations on your success. But it is definitely helpful to plan this expansion in your business plan from the beginning.

Next, let's explore using your product or service in your company name, as this is a popular tactic for many small businesses. There is an upside to instantly resonating with your potential customers on exactly what your business does. For example, Joe's Cupcakes is easily identified as a cupcake shop, possibly owned by someone named Joe. Now the question left with the customer is, who is Joe and do they sell more than just cupcakes? Now it is up to you to decide how you wish to brand your business, and you need to evaluate your competition and your future expansion of your business plan.

Taking this a step forward, the owner of Joe's Cupcakes can create a brand identify with an illustration of "Joe" in the logo and can make the slogan "Cupcakes and Beyond!" Now you have questions answered with your brand imagery. Keep in mind here, Joe's Cupcakes is a fictional company I am just using as an example. And this is an example of a company who would not want to invest large advertising budgets to create brand awareness for a new local cupcake shop. This is why your business plan and expansion ideas would come into play.

Your last option is to decide if you are going to create a word as the name of your business. This is equally as popular as a trend, but will require branding ad campaigns to make your potential customers aware of what your business does. One of the latest trends has been to misspell words, often by removing a vowel, usually for the purpose of creating a unique name that has an available domain for sale.

The availability of domains is the most important factor in naming a company, and is often the most overlooked variable in the equation. I have come up with so many great company names in the past, just to be let down by the domain name being unavailable in domain registrars. This is why I always have a domain registrar search open while I am brainstorming names for businesses. Also understanding that a dot com is far better than dot anything else, at least in speaking for the United States. Dot anything else is easily forgotten, and also is not easily shared through word of mouth advertising.

REGISTERING A DOMAIN NAME

While I am brainstorming business names, I often have my favorite domain registrar company's website open. With each new business name idea, I type into the search function to see if that domain is already taken in a dot com format. As mentioned before, my target is dot com, definitely for the main website. Other landing pages and promotions I can buy dot net, or dot other domains. Lately I have been purchasing dot xyz domains, this following the rebrand of Google to ABC.XYZ. I figured that if dot xyz was good for Google, then it should be good for me to own domains with dot xyz.

Honestly though, the decision is completely up to you and the branding for your business. Over the years, I have worked with massive website companies, and a few of these companies have had issues with copycats. Because of copycats and other potential reputation issues, we started buying up domains in every extension we could get our hands on. And we were also buying misspellings of domains for the main site. Then we would redirect all the domains to the main site. The only purpose of this is that no one else can buy that domain and publish content in competition to the main site, and if someone typed into the search bar with a misspelling, then they would redirect to the main site. Nine out of 10 companies should not worry as much about this, stay focused on the main domain for your business.

I mention all this domain purchasing because that project became very expensive and had very little positive return on investment that could be seen. We attempted to purchase every domain for the main site URL, in every country. Some countries have laws that prohibit such sale, as a business license or offices in that country are required by their laws. In those cases, we skipped those domains. All in all, I do not remember exactly how many domains we purchased, but I do remember that the cost was over $100,000 per year to maintain ownership of hundreds of domains. Some domains require payments of over $200 per year, and some are even higher. I did not believe this was a smart move at the time, and after seeing a zero return on that investment, I can say it was not a good decision still to this day.

If you are operating in a different country, research the domains for your country and be sure to host your website on servers inside your country. This will help with ranking in search engines locally, instead of hosting in a different country and attempting to rank in your country. For example, if you live in the United Kingdom, attempt to buy the domain dot co dot uk. Then try and host your website on systems that are inside of the United Kingdom. Not to say it is impossible to rank a dot com site in the United Kingdom search engines, but search engine optimization is getting more competitive and you need every advantage you can get to beat your competitors.

Without going too deep into search engine optimization strategies in regards to purchasing domains, just remember to purchase the shortest domain name possible, and then maintain that brand throughout all your social media. We have an entire training series in ScaleUP Academy that goes in-depth into search engine optimization and purchasing domains with rankings in mind. Be sure to sign up for ScaleUP Academy and go through our workshops online.

Lastly, don't stay too focused on search engine optimization; however do not avoid search engine optimization and ranking in search engines completely. Often I will set up campaigns that are taking search engine rankings into consideration, just as the icing on the cake for traffic. Meaning, I will use advertising and marketing strategies not attributed to search engines to create 80% of the website traffic, then 20% or so of the website traffic for the site can be from search engines. This is not an exact number for every business, so don't say "Matt says I should have 20% search engine traffic, when it is the opposite and I have 80% of my traffic from search engines."

Fact is, I am just giving examples with numbers from campaigns I have worked on in the past. Some businesses might have a majority of the sales coming from search engines, and that is where attention should be focused, where others have 80% coming from other sources and therefore search engines should not be the focus for your attention.

Again, another strong reason why you need a great business plan, and a mentor who can guide you through these marketing strategies that you might not have had previous experience with testing. Find someone like me who can help guide you through these processes, as they have accomplished and tested ideas before. Leverage our experience to save yourself time and money. More on A/B testing in future chapters.

YOUR LOGO

You found the perfect company name. That's perfect! Now you need a graphic representing that name as your identity for your business. When developing logos, I tap as many designers as possible and there are a few ways to do this. Sites that I have used are 99 Designs, Fiverr, Upwork and other freelancer communities where I can hire for mock-ups. Typically, I will ask for a couple mock-ups per freelancer, and I will ask several freelancers. You will find that most graphic artists have a certain style and often some designer styles can clash with your vision.

Therefore, I typically leverage several designers through different methods and plan to invest a few hundred, if not several thousand dollars looking for the perfect design to match the vision. The secret to extracting the best work from graphic designers is twofold:

1) communicating your vision as clearly and completely as possible
2) giving positive feedback to the designer and being constructive with criticism

We will get more in-depth with team building and how to extract the best from your team in future chapters, but for now realize that the best way to bring out the best in your people is through positive reinforcement. And unless you are a graphic designer, the only way you will have an awesome looking brand identity is if you treat your graphic designer well. Or else you will soon find yourself looking for a new graphic designer.

Now you have a few designs, and you have asked your friends what they like and don't like. You have an idea what you like, but are back and forth on the design. If you are not 100%, go back to the drawing board until you are 100% happy with the design. I know that I have said already in the book that pivoting is OK, but you need to feel good about your logo. The smaller things are not as important, but your logo will need to go on everything. And you need to send out for business cards as soon as possible to get moving.

SOCIAL MEDIA PRESENCE

Typically, I begin with the social media presence quickly, and it is important to keep your brand and voice similar across all platforms. Now with social media graphics, you have to start considering your offers and slogans. We will talk more about copywriting for sales in Chapter 6, but for now we can discuss how to create your messaging across social media.

The best offers are free. If, by chance, you are able to create a free offer, free gift, free workshop or anything free, this is the best way to get someone to take action. The best action is an email list sign up for a free offer. Without getting too ahead of ourselves in talking about sales funnels, understand that our main objective on any page that you have control over will be to get someone to give their name and email address.

Next, you want to be sure to use your social media space to reinforce your slogan or main message. Your slogan should be thoughtful as you have research your competition and customers. From your research, you have created your slogan that solves a problem for your customers and competes in your market-place. One of my favorite slogans is the Geico slogan: "15 minutes could save you 15% or more on your car insurance." Why do I like it so much? Because it has the elements of time, discount and what it is all in the slogan. Your slogan could be the difference between six figures a year and seven figures a year profit in your business.

Lead towards the action you want the user to take. Do not let your website or social media visitor view your page for more than five seconds without understanding the following:

1) Who is this company?
2) What does this company do?
3) Why should I consider this company?
4) What is the next step I should take?

Do you see how many different messages need to be conveyed graphically in less than five seconds? This is why I like the Geico slogan. They have branded the company over the years through television, radio, print and online advertising to immediately understand this message is from Geico. The slogan says "car insurance" in plain text, the company is asking you to consider just for a free quote, and the next step is to take less than 15 minutes out of your day to see if you can save money by switching. This is an example of an amazing slogan and ad campaign, in my opinion.

If you are able to come up with an idea that conveys these points for your business, and you are able to instantly connect with your audience at a glance, then your slogan and social media graphics have done their job correctly. Be sure to track activity before and after the changing of your social media graphics, and note that many companies have seen increases in sales when social media imagery is updated. Always stay top of mind for your customers and potential customers. And social media graphics are a great way to stay connected.

CONSISTENCY

Keep your brand consistent and if you choose to change part of your brand image or your voice, change your image across all platforms. Due to the abundance of options on where to purchase, it is important to keep your customers and website visitors confident they are in the right place. If your website visitors think for a moment that they are in the wrong place, or get an uneasy feeling that the website they are looking at is not where they want to be, they might leave and never return. Keep in mind, a percentage of your visitors will take no action and might never return to your website ever again. Be sure to keep your message clear from the first visit, and stay consistent as you are setting up the customer for a sale or sign up.

Think about your website visitors in this way — they could be a rocket scientist with an IQ topping the scale, a genius. But once someone visits your website, they need to be treated like a fifth-grader. Make everything on your website and social media very simple to understand, so simple that a child could know what to do and what actions to take. The easier your website and social media is to understand and follow along, the higher the success rate of achieving your goals, whether that be a free sign-up, or a purchase of a product.

This is important to keep in mind as the inconsistency on your site can raise questions such as, "Am I in the right place? Is this the company that I was looking at before? Should I wait to purchase?" Typically, people do not remember what they had for breakfast, and they will usually not remember to visit back to your website. If you are not running remarketing campaigns, and if that customer is not already on your email list, there is a chance you can lose them with having inconsistency in your graphics and with your online presence.

PEOPLE ARE PAYING ATTENTION

If you have anything published online, know people are paying attention to your content, even if you think no one is watching. At times, we can forget that people are paying attention to our messaging as we are not getting the likes, comments, shares and feedback that we are looking for. But trust me, there is at least one person taking notice.

Yes, you can and should utilize tracking and reporting at every point in your marketing that you can possibly set up. But every marketing effort does not guarantee reliable reporting. For example, I can see how many video views, website page visits, listens to my podcast, reach for my advertising impressions, and the list goes on. However, I am unable to track eyeballs on television ads, newspaper views and other print media like magazines, radio listens, billboard views and other traditional advertising like direct mail pieces. Perhaps this is one more reason why online marketing is the wave of the future, as reporting on impressions is more realistic in comparison to traditional advertising distribution figures. In this case, if the viewer does not view the page where my ad exists, it is impossible to know.

On the other hand, if I publish videos, blog articles and other content that has received 10 or less views, I should not get discouraged because people could find this media in the future. And yes it is possible to create sales with 10 or less views. Realistically, it only takes 1 view and 1 sale to make a project worth while to me. That would be a 100% success rate, and then I would begin advertising that video or media to grow my viewership; and hopefully growing my sales at the same rate. Understanding that 100% is not sustainable, but it is definitely a great feeling to keep us motivated to continue making new content.

Most of my content does much better in terms of views and sales, but when I started, my viewership and engagement was terrible. Entrepreneurs have quit their businesses after horrible failures like I have had, and I can personally name some friends who have quit on their dreams. It is sad, but again, not everyone is ready for success. But it is never too late to get started building your dreams.

So I continue to press on, getting better and better with every post that I publish, and learning how the pros got started and built their networks. I keep pushing on and sales keep rolling in. For those of you who tried once and failed, the only way no one will purchase is if you stop posting and stop testing new ideas. If you keep working at your talent and continue pressing forward, know that people are paying attention and they will take action. Just keep moving.

THE SEVEN PILLARS

PILLAR 5

CHAPTER 5

LEVERAGING TECHNOLOGY

The most valuable commodity that you have is your time. You cannot buy more time and there is no monetary value that you can exchange to buy more time. As you begin to realize this, you will begin to evaluating how you approach your business in regards to your time. Understanding that no one gets rich from hourly work, unless you are charging a very large sum per hour. Six figures a year in revenue is simple, as you can sell your time.

40 hours a week X 4 weeks per month X 12 months per year = 1920 hours

Divide 1920 hours by $100,000 and you will get $52.08

Therefore, for this example, if you charge $75 per hour, you should easily reach six figures in gross revenue.

For years, my hourly rate was $100. Other streams of income pushed my earnings over $100,000 per year in revenue, but that is not seven figures. Here is what I would have had to charge at an hourly rate to earn seven figures:

$1,000,000 divided by 1920 hours = $521 per hour

Who is going to pay $521 per hour for marketing for one year? Not many companies would ever consider hiring a freelance marketer and pay this sum on an hourly wage. Now this does not take into consideration commissions that can be written into contracts. Performance-based incomes can easily reach over seven figures with the right business plan. But perhaps you're a lawyer and can charge a premium for your time, but you are not billing a full 1,920 hours per year. You need to leverage technology and monetize the system.

There are so many ways to systematize and leverage technology to grow your wealth, but the most popular is to create a product. You can also grow a team and charge a premium for time, where you pay your team a lower rate than the client is billed. In both instances, you can leverage technology to systematize your sales process, inbound marketing and fulfillment, or you can choose to leverage technology for productivity and duplication of service where the client pays a premium and the staff members earn salary.

I have developed products, both digital and physical, and sold services, attempting to duplicate myself. Unfortunately, no one is as good as I am in providing services for clients, and had to back off on bringing on more clients and training more staff. I felt that sacrificing quality was not worth increasing clients, and therefore I created a digital product in my training to ensure every member received the same level of service and customer care. I'm not saying all companies are like mine. I just chose to move towards scaling back my business without hiring a large staff for client work.

Going beyond the training, we are working to certify other consultants through our community to help clients with the development and marketing consulting that they need as they move through the Million Dollar Plan training and ScaleUP Academy. This is my focus, and this plan has allowed me to free up my time to continue creating training materials and books for our customers to leverage and take their businesses to the next level.

If I were to spoon-feed the knowledge that exists through the Million Dollar Plan and ScaleUP Academy to a client, we would need more than 1,000 hours for me to teach the client everything that is learned through the training. Do I have members who have gone through the training who would rather pay me $1 million or more per year for me to execute this for their businesses? The answer is actually YES! We are currently working with clients now who have offered us large sums, plus revenue share in their businesses. This is the only business model we will work from going forward, as the demand on our time has overpassed the hours in a day.

Why am I mentioning this? Because you need to take your time and the demand into consideration. As I started earning millions for companies, my time was taken from me in the form of hourly rate, which did not earn the revenues that I needed to achieve my goals. The only way for me to work for a client and achieve my goals at the same time is through hourly rate, plus revenue share of the sales. These clients held me back from launching my business and achieving my greatness for years as I worked diligently building other companies. When I learned that the sacrifice of my time would not allow me to achieve my goals, I began researching how to sell my knowledge in order to scale myself.

SALE OF PRODUCTS

There are so many different ways to sell products, and I am earning through almost every method possible. This book is a product that was created, put on Amazon and now I earn royalties from sales each month. I also have physical products that are in Amazon warehouses, that is if I haven't already sold out those companies. I have created digital products that I sell through ScaleUP Academy, and I also have software that is being sold through my websites. Some programs are on monthly subscriptions and others are lifetime purchases.

Beyond the sale of products mentioned above, I have also partnered with other entrepreneurs who sell real estate where I am earning commissions from house sales and other various companies that I earn revenue shares. Selling products and finding better ways to sell products is how so many of the top companies have earned millions and billions. If you are able to identify market opportunities to sell products better or easier, there is potential for your business to step into a space that can generate a fortune for you and your employees.

For example, one of my digital products sold for $1,497. In order to achieve seven figures, I had to sell 669 orders. This sales volume is totally possible to achieve every month, based upon the market opportunity of entrepreneurs looking for training. Seven figures a month as a solo entrepreneur, charging an hourly rate is impossible. But selling seven figures a month in a digital product and books is possible. Not only possible, but there are countless entrepreneurs who are actively selling over seven figures a month!

In order to achieve your goal, you must reconsider how you leverage your time, verses leveraging the technology to grow your business and sales. Technology can be used for more than just creating digital products. You can also leverage your system for fulfillment, customer service systems and even assistance with productivity.

INFORMATION PRODUCTS

The sale of information or your expertise is the holy grail of passive income in regards to scaling your time. The benefit of selling an information product is that the development of your product could take 40 hours of your time, for example. Yet you could sell this product 1,000 times over, every year, forever. The financial benefits of selling an information product can be very lucrative; however, the greatest benefit is that you can craft your product around something that you love.

Create a life and a business that you love, set your schedule and enjoy what you do for work every day; all while helping people in their lives. Think of an information product as a win-win for everyone. Unfortunately, entrepreneurs will approach their product with the wrong approach. Those who are too focused on the lifestyle, cars, yachts, mansions and freedom often lose sight of what truly matters - helping people solve their problems. If you are able to identify a need in the marketplace, and your expertise is in high demand, consider making an information product to help people with their issues.

There are so many different ways to deliver an information product, and equally as many ways to attract new customers to your business. Like always, the first place that I begin brainstorming the launch of an information product is by looking at the competition. Or if there is no direct competition, I look for people who have already launched a similar product. Typically, when I am looking through blogs, videos, books, podcasts and other media, I let my mind begin to explore taking the approach of the competitor but introducing my new spin on the concept.

Keeping in mind, the best way to stand out is to be the best at something, and brand yourself as the best in that field. Think about it this way: would you go to a surgeon that only works on hands for hand surgery, or would you rather hire a surgeon who specializes in any aliment? Same goes for your customers when considering who to purchase from online. Your potential customers in your space are advertised to hundreds if not thousands of times a day. Your ads will need to stand out, and your message will need to be embedded into their minds. Understand face-to-face meetings stick in the mind longer than a video or blog that was read. Leave a lasting impression as your first impression.

Perhaps the most difficult objective with selling information products is to convince your potential customer that you are, in fact, an expert. The issue here is that you need to predict what the viewer will be thinking and what they want from the beginning. A majority of traffic to your message could be generated online with an advertisement; and from that first ad, you need to be focused on what their objections will be. In future chapters we will discuss copywriting, sales funnels and the psychology of online sales.

A simple phone call can often help to overcome online objectives. People want to feel like their questions are all being answered, that you are in fact an expert, and lastly this information product is for them. If they can realize all of these objectives and approach the sales page feeling good about the next step, there is an excellent chance they will consider purchasing your product. Again, we focus on taking your time out of the equation to the best of our abilities, but we also understand there might be 10 out of 100 interested buyers who just want to talk to a human before buying. Later this chapter we discuss more in detail systematization and leveraging online systems to qualify leads.

If you are considering launching your own information product, be sure to join ScaleUP Academy today, where we take you step-by-step through the process of creating your product from idea to planning to launch and success!

SALE OF SERVICES

Leveraging technology is also required when choosing to grow your business by selling a service. I have worked on projects using our systems to recruit and train new staff. We will then use those same systems to attract prospects, make them customers and then round-robin the new clients into a project manager to handle the services. These systems were built to manage the criteria, as well as assigning the customer to a staff member based off geographical data and the needs indicated by the customer.

These systems can include surveys and other questionnaires that qualify the needs of the new customer within the sales process, and will move the customer into the service that best suits their requirements. Without leveraging these systems, we would destroy our profits by having to hire more staff to manage the phones, calling each new customer in the sales or questionnaire process that is otherwise handled by the coding of our system, which can be managed by a single programmer. In short, one programmer can manage the sale to millions of customers, and without the system created, we would need hundreds of customer service reps to handle these phone calls to new customers.

In your business, staff will come and go; therefore your training system needs to be top notch to get your new staff members up to speed on fulfilling services. Without the training content, the cost for training each staff member is estimated at $20,000 per person. By leveraging online training, plus a certification system, we can build systems for the cost of training one person. These training systems can be managed at the cost of training two additional people per year. By leveraging technology for training staff and certification processes, we can train 1,000 or more staff members per month for an affordable cost. Without leveraging technology, this would not be possible without completely removing our profits from the bottom line.

Don't rule out services as a sustainable business model for generating seven and eight figures for your business. However, leverage technology to train staff, manage customer service and fulfill services through as much automation as possible. The more you can systematize in your business, the more wealth you can generate for your company.

SALES PROCESS

It is easy to understand how your technology build can automate aspects of generating sales through your website. However, also take into consideration that your systems can weed out potential bad clients and customers. For example, say you're in the real estate business. It is safe to assume that you would agree that time is definitely not on your side. And your time is valuable.

Potential real estate clients need to be qualified, as you cannot put a buy now button on your website to have million-dollar real estate deals happen, or even a $100,000 deal. There is no way to generate sales through eCommerce. Perhaps maybe one day in the future you can buy a home with a click from a website, and have $1 million leave your bank account, but that day is not today. So how does a real estate agent value their time? By weeding out unqualified customers. Unfortunately, this process can become time consuming through phone calls and meeting in person to qualify your buyers.

Here is where leveraging online questionnaires to qualify potential buyers or sellers can help maximize productivity. But keep in mind, it is nearly impossible to guarantee that every customer or potential client will fill out questionnaires with 100% honesty, but you can still ask the tough questions via online systems that can eliminate those clients who would have otherwise consumed your valuable time. In working with real estate professionals over the years, the biggest issue they have is spending time with clients looking up MLS listings and even taking clients around to see properties before they are qualified.

The qualification of a potential client before time is exchanged applies to businesses other than just real estate, as that was only an example. In fact, it applies to my business now, but there was a time in the past where I would spend a half hour on the phone with just about anyone. At one time in my life, I was spending hours a day on the phone with potential clients, chasing existing clients for content, feedback and payments for work rendered, and I was also trying to find time to actually do the programming and development work. Insane to think how I was spending my time unwisely, and spinning my wheels, just squeaking by. I can say with confidence, my business would have completely failed if it wasn't for automating processes and leveraging technology.

Understand that is what happens when you are hungry and will do anything to make a sale and for some, just accomplish staying in business. But once you realize that your time is valuable, and you start taking your time more seriously by leveraging technology to qualify leads, then this miraculous thing happens and you spend more time working with good leads and less time on the unqualified leads. Another thing can also happen, with a steady stream of qualified leads, you will feel more confident charging higher prices so you get paid what your time is actually worth. Now this doesn't go for every industry, but there are thousands of other freelancers who are living from project to project, waiting for their breakout success. I was once on that level.

Also remember that when you treat your time as being more valuable, it is incredible to watch how your clients and prospective clients will begin to treat your time as more valuable as well. Use technology to stay productive, stick to schedules and keep your focus. Then you are maximizing productivity while valuing your most valuable resource.

YOUR MACHINE

Building your machine takes time and resources, but if you build it correctly the first time, it is possible that you will never have to revisit development again. Create your plan, identify your audience, their frustrations, your competitors and your unique value proposition or offer for your potential customers, and then go to work.

When developing your online marketing machine, either start at the cash register or your lead magnet/offer. For me, I like to start with the cash register and work backwards. I will use a project now that I am working on as an example: ScaleUP Media's Best-Selling Author Training for $997.

My plan is to sell this $997 course after the potential client watches an hour-long free workshop, which I plan on stacking some bonus offers if they buy within a limited time. We will get into sales copy that sells in the next chapter. This free workshop will show how I have launched best-selling books in X weeks, and have case studies along with other awesome free information.

In order to attract these viewers of the free workshop, I will need to advertise an offer through Facebook, and can attract potential customers who are interested in self-publishing through a variety of different Facebook Ad targets. Now I will need a great landing page to go along with the ad that offers a free case study and workshop for seeing how to launch a number one best seller.

Between the initial sign-up and the free workshop, I need to work on some emails that will reinforce reasons to attend my workshop. This can include added incentives, bonus content or videos and the fear of loss. Again, we will go in-depth into copy that sells in the next chapter. For now, the main focus is to understand how I am leveraging technology to create leads, and then qualify the leads before they are pitched to become customers.

For example, let's run some numbers. With Facebook ads, I am able to put my marketing message and page in front of 10,000 interested or prospective authors using Facebook interest targeting. Out of the 10,000 people seeing impressions of ads, I receive 3,000 clicks and 1,300 sign-ups on the landing page. I now have 1,300 people who said they were interested and shared their email addresses with my system. Of those 1,300 people interested, 700 show up for my free online workshop or the replay of the workshop. That is 700 people who hear my voice, my message, offer and pitch in a single day.

Ordinarily with an hour-long presentation and sales pitch, it would take 700 or more hours to educate and deliver my offer to 700 people. In an 8-hour workday, I would need 88 employees making back-to-back sales calls every hour for 8 hours in order to reach 700 people. From these 700 people, I am now able to use my email marketing follow-up sequences, which are all automated to identify the user's statuses: not interested at all, somewhat interested and want to hear more, or ready to buy.

Let's say 400 people were not interested in all. I could then offer another free workshop in the next 14 days, but if no action is taken, I will remove them completely off my list. Again, this process is completely automated by my systems. And the thought process here is to offer a lower priced item, or attempt to see if they are interested in something else I offer. Considering the fact that I promised to never spam or sell their information, I would rather keep my promise than sell that lead. However, some businesses at this point choose to sell unresponsive leads for a profit, but for me, I honor my promises and keep my integrity intact by never selling customer information.

The 50 users who are interested can purchase through the system right away and gain access to the product. This leaves 250 people who are interested, but something held them back. Using email marketing automation, my systems will continue to educate and offer bonuses until they decide to buy or not. In this sequence, I can identify the people who might want to talk to a live person. Eureka! By leveraging technology, I was able to whittle down a list of 700 people down to 20 or so who would like to talk on the phone for 10 to 15 minutes. I just saved hundreds of hours leveraging marketing automation and technology.

LEVERAGING INFUSIONSOFT

Without getting too technical, let's talk technology for a moment and the software Infusionsoft. Keep in mind, everything explained in this entire book is covered in detail through ScaleUP Academy. And we have an entire training series dedicated to leveraging Infusionsoft. OK, so what is this software?

Before I get too in-depth into explaining the software that is the backbone of my and many of my clients' businesses, let me first tell you the history of how I came to love this software.

In 2003, I was building websites and had no idea how to make a website functional. Let's face it, I was lucky if all the pages in the menu loaded correctly. Fast forward a few years when I was starting to leverage email marketing and was introduced to MailChimp. It blew my mind! I could embed a little bit of code and then capture email addresses to send emails to my subscribers.

Around 2005, I started learning how to monetize my new found talents of Internet marketing, but still there were aspects of tracking and reporting that were completely missing from the equation. Not to mention, eCommerce websites were still beyond my knowledge. I began learning how to manipulate my site to rank in search engines, and found that I was growing my online presence through the limited tools that I had available.

When comparing my vast knowledge of systems and technology today to my knowledge in 2007, it brings a smile to my face. I wish I knew then what I know now! Since I do not have a time machine, we can only speculate what would have happened in my life if I had this book as a guide back then. Regardless, I took the knowledge that I had and started a web agency.

All the work I was doing was labor intensive, spending hours at a computer. I was spending too much time on every project, every bit of code that I was implementing took forever to troubleshoot and I was fumbling through projects. This love for building the future of the web took me on a journey to live in New York City in 2009, and I started work for one of the top 200 most visited websites.

There I learned about this thing called a CRM, customer relationship management system. This company custom built a system that managed sales, marketing, reporting, customer support and everything wrapped into one robust system. Also, the company leveraged sales funnels and taught me how to write copy for sales. This experience was priceless, and I worked with that company for five years!

Midway through my career with this massive web company, I had my breakthrough idea. I need to help smaller companies implement similar software solutions like the bigger companies. But where are these applications and are they affordable? Enter Infusionsoft!

Think of Infusionsoft as the engine of your car, or the backbone of your business. Your customers will never see it, but it is making your car run. After implementing this software into my business, sales started coming in at a faster rate! Why? The eCommerce and follow-up sequences were so simple to set up that I had built out an entire sales funnel process in an hour or so.

What took me weeks, using MailChimp for emails and PayPal for payment days, was now taking hours. And let's remember that time is the most valuable commodity that we have. The intricate functions we were implementing through my former client's custom built CRM system could be handled through the Infusionsoft simple campaign builder. Thank goodness for drag and drop templates! I do not like wasting my time with code, and I am a visual builder. Infusionsoft has been a game changer for my business.

Is Infusionsoft the only software that does all this? No. But I have tested a few other solutions and am sticking with Infusionsoft. Will I stay with the software forever? Perhaps! So many entrepreneurs are held back because they are constantly building and rebuilding, always chasing the new technology. Something new comes out, and they completely rebuild their system over. This will get you nowhere. So yes, I will stick with Infusionsoft for a long while to run my business on autopilot.

Fact is, there will always be new software systems, and if you are able to stay away from the "shiny new object syndrome," then you will be able to be more productive. There are entrepreneurs today who spend the hours to build their systems, then tweak for performance; and when the system is finely tuned, they will let their systems run forever! In fact, a few entrepreneurs are still using the same systems they set up in 2009! That is six years of using the same setup, and this structure will keep you focused more on advertising and building traffic rather than consistently tinkering with your machine.

POWER OF EVERGREEN

In botany, an evergreen is a plant that has leaves throughout the year, always green. In marketing, evergreen has a bit different meaning but in some ways is similar, always green. The thought process is simple - build a system, watch the reports as your traffic begins to come to the site, and then tweak the system to maximize performance. Once the system is optimized, then you flip the switch to go live and will let the system run, possibly forever.

I believe in innovative entrepreneurs, and there are so many examples of software systems that have been built by entrepreneurs who had specific needs in their businesses. An excellent example of this is with the development of WebinarJam and EverWebinar. These software programs power my webinars and online workshops for my members. Within these programs, I am able to set up my marketing automation and presentations. Webinar software and other online video presentation software has existed for years, and several giant software companies developed solutions. However, these solutions were not good enough, and a couple entrepreneurs identified a need, and provided a software as a solution.

Within many of these software solutions is the ability for a solo-entrepreneur or someone with limited resources to run their own marketing campaigns. Think about that, software that has been built from the ground up with non-technical minded people as the targeted users for the systems. No, I am not personally able to open a blank document and build a complete software program from scratch. But what I am able to do is learn how to set up software systems that other people have created, and connect those systems through API (application program interface) solutions. API in layman's terms means software programs talking to each other and executing functions based on another program's protocols.

When building a system, I look for the software that will accomplish the tasks, and each piece of software needs to communicate through API with the other systems I already have in place. Now I also look for software systems that can be set up easily and can run evergreen where the systems are generating revenues for the company without having to be hands-on. If the system requires manual actions, I try to automate as much as possible, while still maintaining an excellent user experience. If the user experience would be sacrificed in the usage of the evergreen software systems, then I would reconsider the usage of those systems for my solutions.

In short, do not set up software solutions that frustrate your members, viewers or customers. If the software that you are setting up is creating a bad user experience and you are seeing an increase in complaints, then you will need to make changes to the software systems to give the highest levels of customer care. To me, a great customer experience is more important than increased revenues, but if I am able to leverage evergreen systems and at the same time create happy customers, well then we have a win-win situation! That is the sweet spot.

SCARCITY SELLS

When building online systems that sell, scarcity is the most important aspect of the online sales process. In the next chapter we will dig into copy writing for sales in detail, however for now we need to discuss the scarcity systems that you will set up for your web pages and evergreen systems.

Scarcity on sales pages or sign-up pages can be seen in two different ways - in text or graphically. An example of a scarcity graphic could be a countdown timer that is counting down to the end of an offer. And in text, the scarcity can appear in the form of saying "limited time offer" or "limited to the first 100 customers." An excellent example of this is on QVC or any home shopping network, or perhaps going back to the infomercials on TV that we love. "Be one of the first 100 callers and you will receive this excellent bonus!"

With these scarcity messages, we can convey a fear of loss where the viewer could miss out if they do not act right away. To some people this sales tactic is slimy and feels wrong. But for those of us who own the company, and it is our marketing message, we can set up the scarcity sale without losing our integrity in the sales process. One great example of this is Ticketmaster. As you select your seats for the event, a countdown timer is letting you know that you will lose these seats if you are unable to complete the purchase in time.

Keep in mind as you are setting up your offers to give an expiration date. If the system is set up correctly, you will have a majority of your sales happen on first visit, and then the other bulk of sales happen on the last day. It is important to use software that is correctly counting down for the user or counting down to the last day in the process, then have your email marketing reflect the correct timing in the process. If you do this correctly, the scarcity and limited time offers can drive your sales through the roof, but if you set this up incorrectly, you could potentially find yourself with more customer service problems.

For those of you who want to see the scarcity countdown in action, join ScaleUP Academy, and depending on the messaging and how the offer of the week is set up, we might currently have a countdown timer running. For those of you would want to implement scarcity in your business, go forward with a ScaleUP Academy membership and you will see exactly how we set up scarcity timers, the follow up messages and the copy that will drive higher sales for your offers.

LEVERAGING PARTNERSHIPS

Partnerships can be a great way to grow your business and your influence quickly. With partnerships, you can leverage the network and credibility from your partners to generate sales rapidly. Before you get worried about giving up equity, know that partnerships in marketing could mean a joint venture or co-branding of a sales page. The top marketers run these campaigns frequently, and I will go into detail here on how you can leverage partnerships to grow your business.

Most of the people who start a business, or are just getting started growing a business do not have a large list of engaged customers in their email system. In some cases, we have worked with authors or business owners who already have an established customer base for buying books, then the idea is to take this audience and put them into online training and workshops. However, for those who are getting started with a small list and advertising budget, leveraging partnerships can be a great way to grow an engaged audience very quickly.

How do you find these partners? That is a really great question! The best way to meet new potential partners is at trade shows and other events in your industry. Meet and exchange information with as many people as possible. First build a relationship, and over time begin to suggest the partnership for revenue sharing. Keep in mind, most of the people who have large lists of engaged users will typically hold that list as their most valued possession. And the last thing they would want is to cross-sell your products then have you pester their list with your sales copy till they unsubscribe.

Now you might say, "what about the people who just mail other offers?" Keep in mind, you want a partner who has a list with a high open rate, and a high click and sale rate for the 'right' products. There is no point putting eyeballs on an offer that never converts to a sale for your business; you cannot take 'exposure' down to the grocery store and buy eggs. We are in the business to create leads and make sales; with that, never buy email lists and think that you can mail. There is the unicorn chance of having success, but don't risk it. You can find your website banned, IP address banned, get yourself banned from your mailing system and also find yourself having to focus on reputation management due to poor performing email marketing campaigns.

So now you found the perfect partner, where your product or service fits nicely into their audience. Now what? First step is to strike the deal, and get this in writing. After you get your partnership agreement in writing, it is time to begin building your campaign. There are a couple great ways to approach advertising this offer, and my favorite is a co-branded online workshop. The number one reason people buy is because they are educated customers and they know what they want and why they want it. And a great way to do this is by creating a workshop where the list owner will send mail to his or her list, informing the customer about an upcoming free workshop where they will learn about something that might interest them. You will also be present at this workshop to introduce your product, educating the viewer and then pitching your offer at the end of the presentation. Think of this process as an invitation to pitch your offer to an audience, and you have their attention throughout the presentation.

There are several ways that you can handle this workshop, but the best way is by using WebinarJam or EverWebinar, two products that we highly recommend for educating and selling to your audience. In this example, you will have the opportunity to leverage a partner's list and you will have their full attention, depending on the quality of the list and their trust of the list owner. Are you starting to see why you need to find the right partnership and the right opportunities?

Set up a few great partnerships (JV campaigns), and the door can open to a new world of possibilities for your business. Once you create a successful campaign, then you will have the ability to sell other partners very quickly on your opportunity or offer. If your offer is hot, and new partners see your offer as an opportunity to sell to their list, they will jump on the offer and bundle their products up as bonuses for buying through their partner links. Think about it this way, your product becomes the "talk of the town" and then you will have partners competing to have their list buy your product. Also keeping in mind that once you get into sharing lists, and cross-selling offers, these partner's lists could be very similar, with lots of familiar faces on each other's lists. Taking this a step further, if the customer is on multiple lists, then they have bought multiple offers, and with that, they are the prime candidates for pitching the offers.

Let's break all this down into numbers: you could partner with someone who has 100,000 emails on their list, and of the 100,000, let's say 20,000 have purchase something for $5 or more; 8,000 have purchased a product for $500 or more, and the lifetime value of 2,000 on the list is over $5,000 in sales. Therefore, the partner might decide to offer the part of their list who have never purchased anything, which is not the best deal for your offer. For your success, you will want to negotiate the offer being seen by the best customers on the list. Also, understand that the best customers are probably on other lists. Therefore, they will be seeing the same offer over and over from different partners.

Your goal is to find the right partners, develop relationships with them, and start small with your offers, slowly educating the partner's list about your products and services. With time, you can grow your list with the best clients from other's lists who perhaps spent a premium to create their list through their advertising campaigns. By following this concept, you can save thousands of dollars in advertising because the best customers, who have already purchased, are a couple clicks away from being introduced to your product.

At this time, you are thinking, "oh yes! I want partnerships right now!" Not so fast! The best way to sell a partnership is with a proven product and proven case studies for driving sales through your presentations and your offers. Therefore, you might be putting the cart before the horse jumping right into partnering for a JV product launch. Start testing the waters and perfecting your offers before approaching potential partners. You will only get one first impression, make it count.

ALWAYS CLOSING SALES

At any moment, any day of the week, at any time of the day, there is someone considering purchasing one of my products. And with any luck from my excellent sales pages, there are sales being generated every hour of every day throughout the entire year. This is the end goal of owning an online business, and passive income is a goal that we are all striving to achieve.

But what exactly does passive income mean? I no longer think in terms of creating "passive income" versus whatever you would consider the opposite. I now think in terms of creating sales machines, and then sending as much traffic through the machine as possible. With this mindset, I am in the business of building machines, then setting up reporting for tracking sales. After one machine is built, I move onto the next project. Once you are able to set up a program and trade quarters in advertising for dollars in sales, then you have a system that is generating passive income.

In my younger years, I thought that passive income had to be achieved through multi-level marketing or network marketing businesses. Then I thought that passive income was achieved through blogging and ranking in search engines. Throughout the years, I was able to make a considerable amount of money in both business models; however, I eventually discovered these business models were not sustainable for me. Don't get me wrong, I know several business owners who are doing very well in these industries, but for most of us, these industries are not sustainable. And to me, I want to build, test, tweak and pivot towards success, and then not have to touch the machine unless for a small bit of maintenance.

If you do not own your business and every aspect of the system, it can be taken away from you. I have seen network marketing companies go out of business, and I have had websites that were ranking in the top of search engines lose interest. In fact, I had a website that ranked on the top of search engines for months, creating millions of page views and organic website visitors. After I put a few ads on the page, I was able to earn ad revenue checks over $10,000 a month! It was insane. And I thought this was my future, I finally found what I do really well, ranking websites in Google. Well, so do thousands of other people like me, and it is a dog-eat-dog world out there where you always have to look out for the next best opportunity.

I don't want to continue chasing my tail, and I do not want a virus or malware on a web server to put me out of business. How do I continue expanding myself as a serial entrepreneur, but at the same time, build a steady foundation for years of earnings? Answer: provide value!

Enter information products, writing books and building software solutions! Yes, I have achieved passive income, and I have built systems that automate my sales processes, fulfillment and training for my customers. Over the years, I have learned how to test, track, pivot and scale the strategies that thousands of entrepreneurs and wantrapreneurs are looking for online. Wantrapreneurs by definition are those people who want to become an entrepreneur, talk about starting a business, and buy training but never actually get started. Don't be a wantrapreneur.

Back to always closing, learn the secrets from ScaleUP Academy and my other training courses on how to build your business online, grow your audience and become an expert in your field. I have trained thousands of experts throughout the years, in a variety of different niches. And keep in mind, no niche is too big or too small for you to get started building your influence. Do not worry about having too much competition or not enough competitors. If you truly believe in yourself, your message and believe that you can succeed, then you should stick with your dreams, no matter what. Do not be afraid to pivot on your dreams, but always move towards your goals. Do not let anyone tell you that you are not good enough, or that you cannot achieve creating a sales machine for your idea. Remember, the only person holding you back is you, so get started building your dream today!

THE SEVEN PILLARS

PILLAR 6

CHAPTER 6

COPY THAT SELLS

W e can talk all day about technology, likes on Facebook, rankings in Google and all sorts of other pieces to the Million Dollar Plan, but you will never achieve millionaire status if you are not able to write copy that sells.

You can hire the best WordPress expert, Infusionsoft partner, Facebook and SEO ninja, but if you are unable to write sales copy that moves your potential customers to take out their credit cards and purchase something from you, you're not going to make it to the next level.

All the top influencers and business owners write most of their own copy and create their own content. Now I understand that you can have someone like me get up to speed with your business and help you write copy, eventually. But you need to clearly communicate your business to the freelance copywriter, and you need to set a standard for your business.

Don't roll your eyes copywriters of the world. It is true and you know it! Those clients who are horrible at giving direction and have no idea what they want or how to articulate their offers in writing are typically some of the most difficult clients to work with. On the other hand, those clients who have an idea and bring you onboard to help grow your talents into the business, now you have an active business owner taking the business to new heights.

For years I have struggled with clients, as they think they can hand off a project to me completely, without any copy or direction, and then expect me to live inside their head from day 1. Nope, I am not a mind reader. I am just a guy who knows how to put myself in the prospective audience's shoes and read text on pages through the consumer's eyes. I can predict the prospect's frustrations, and leveraging the best copywriting techniques you are about to learn, I am able to convert a high percentage of website visitors to leads and sales.

TIP 1: DISGUISE YOUR SALES PITCH

The best copywriter will write sales copy without the reader knowing they are reading a pitch. Sales pitches will turn off new website visitors. However, there is a time and place for creating a real sales pitch, and that is right before you are about to remove them from your email list. But you do not want your prospect to read a heavy sales pitch on their first couple visits.

The objective of the first visit is to introduce the reader to your message and what you do, tell your story and let your reader get to know your purpose. Feel free to not link to anything requiring entering of a payment method, as sometimes this can turn off a potential customer. Let the prospect feel comfortable first. Then continue to educate your reader and give them value. VALUE VALUE VALUE! Keep it coming! This is how you begin to create a raving fan.

Then begin to disguise offers in the form of free gifts and other valuable tools that will help them with their frustrations. This is inching towards earning trust and building your rapport with the new or prospective customer. This is a fine balance between giving value and creating solutions, without losing their interest and attention. After the first couple emails and a few videos I have shared, I begin moving into providing downloads or other free workshops.

While on workshops and other training, we offer taking the opportunity to the next level. Make your customers feel comfortable, because let's face it, no one like a used car salesman pitch! Online consumers are getting smarter, and they are getting alerted to the tricks that once worked, so be sure to test the newest tactic, content marketing and giving your customers huge value! Then retarget the potential buyer through ads to give a free workshop or something else that you can give away for free. Wait till you have their undivided attention and move towards your sales pitch, without being too pushy.

TIP 2: STOP READERS IN THEIR TRACKS

The Internet is a massive space and your message can easily get lost in a hurry. Unlike that billboard that you can place on the side of the road where your target prospect will see the ad every day on their way to work, the Internet is an ever-changing landscape that can look different with each click of the refresh button. In Facebook, it is nearly impossible to go find an ad if you missed it on the first go-around, and you will have to hope the ad reaches you again.

Create urgency, stand out with your graphics and be sure your copy headlines are clear and make sense. Stay away from click-bait and other techniques to get clicks fast. These tactics come and go, and you are better building your business on a sustainable foundation. Disrupt their lives and enter your message, plucking the strings that frustrate your audience and allow your target audience to understand at a glance, "This is what I need. This is what I have been looking for."

Again, it is tough to tell you the exact text that will get your prospective audience to stop in their tracks and take action with your site, but you should be testing several different titles and copy to see what works for your business. Always test new ideas!

TIP 3: COLLECT AN EMAIL ADDRESS

New social media fads will come and go, but email marketing is here to stay. Be sure to focus your main action on your site to sign up to an email list. Offer free gifts, free workshops, free anything, or even coupons and discounts to gain a new email sign-up. Your email list should be driving a large percentage of the sales for your business every month. And if you are not driving in sales through your email marketing, get started on that today!

We can go super in-depth into call to actions, but it would be easier for you to join ScaleUP Academy and we can work on that through our training workshops. Keep testing lead magnets and new call to actions to get sign-ups. If the first call to action or lead magnet does not work, keep testing new strategies.

TIP 4: GIVE THEM AN OFFER THEY CAN'T REFUSE

I could write an entire book just on writing sales copy, but if there is just one thing that you take from this chapter, that would be value stacking and reframing. When I learned these strategies to closing sales and the partial takeaway sale, it changed my business forever.

Here is an example: How much would you be willing to pay to generate an extra $1 million in sales for your business next year? $100,000? $50,000? $10,000? What if I told you that clients have worked with us and paid over six figures a year for our services! Don't get me wrong, they are totally happy as their businesses and lives have been changed forever. But what if I told you that our new product is here, and for the next 30 minutes, I will offer you lifetime access to our new system for only $997! As a bonus, I want to throw in a lifetime membership to this and that for free! Just for you taking action today. This package is valued at over $150,000, and you can get all this for only $997.

This is an example of an awesome close you could add to the end of your next workshop or webinar, and by giving huge value throughout the entire presentation, you will have a percentage of your viewers go get their credit card and buy on the spot! There are people right now doing over $1 million in sales per month with this strategy! It's insane to think about. How would you like to do $1 million per month in sales for a product that is completely evergreen? Crazy to think about, right? Sitting on the beach for the month, while watching money come rolling into your bank account. If this is your dream, then make it happen!

Let's go back to the first tip for a moment. If you are able to hide a sales pitch like the one above without the user feeling like they are being pitched by a used car salesman, then you have a game changer for your business. Especially in an evergreen sales process, where the only interaction they have with you is through your email marketing, blog content and videos. Just remember to be sincere with your marketing copy throughout the entire process.

TIP 5: LEAD WITH CASE STUDIES

Learn how a 32-year-old college dropout, who failed ninth-grade English, launched a number one best-selling book in five weeks! That might be a good headline that works for me on a case study video that I will be launching soon, or perhaps it is a different bit of copy. Regardless, these headlines get attention!

Other forms of attention grabbers are using "even if" in your headlines. This tactic is a great way to get attention from your audience and identify with their frustrations. Here is a headline that built my email list to over 5,000 subscribers in three weeks:

"How to rank on page 1 of Google, even if you failed a computer class"

Yes, this headline built my first 5,000 subscribers to my list, and also helped to sell hundreds of SEO courses. One subject line beat out every other test. This headline instantly identifies with website owners and tells them you do not have to be an expert in computers to follow along. This was an awesome product launch and my first huge success in selling an information product online. All thanks to this awesome headline!

Another way to share a case study is by using a download of a blueprint, where you are telling the potential customer to grab your cheat sheet or blueprint that helped you achieve a goal in a certain amount of time. With this form of download, or case study, you will be able to implant the thought of the future success inside the mind of your potential customer before they have seen a sales page. Think about that, you are planting the thought of success with sharing a case study right from the beginning.

Fact is, case studies are not just limited to businesses. They can be used in relatively every form of business. Health, finance, real estate, legal, and the list goes on. As I am sitting here typing this, I cannot think of a single business where a case study would not be helpful. Even in gaming or mobile gaming, there are testimonials or reviews for how others enjoyed the application or game. Insane to think, we are all just followers who take action based upon reading others who have tried and tested before us. Don't fight it, case studies work. We have evolved over the years by learning from previous mistakes.

TIP 6: LIMITED TIME OFFER

The fear of loss is one of the number one drivers of sales for every company. This fear can be conveyed through an expiring offer, a countdown clock on the page, or by explaining how the offer or coupon is only valid for a limited time.

This form of sales can be seen dozens of times a day, through online and offline marketing campaigns. When you become aware of 'limited time offer' sales tactics, they will seem more prevalent in your life. However, keep in mind that when you are looking for something, it will appear more often. Or at least have the perception in your mind that it will appear more frequently. But in fact, limited time offers have been driving copy since the beginning of advertising.

Subliminally our minds are drawn to colors and text that give us the sense of urgency and make us want to take action. Yes, color has been proven to affect our buying habits by changing our mood, making us hungry and in some cases, even raising our blood pressure. Accompany that with a great limited time offer and now you have an excellent sales page. In order to become a great copywriter, open your eyes to the sales campaigns that you see around you.

Your sales will skyrocket when you learn how to utilize the takeaway sale and inject the fear of loss into the mind of your customers. I listen to my friends and family consistently use this fear of loss as to why they compulsively purchased something. "The offer was for today only, so I bought four of them." It makes me laugh thinking this is someone overcoming their buyer's remorse by regurgitating a sales pitch that was cooked up by some marketer.

A great place to see how people react to sales copy and offers is inside department stores. Keep in mind, this book is mostly focused on leveraging online sales, but it is tough to visualize the website visitor sitting at home, and it is much easier to see how people interact inside a physical store. Watch how people are attracted to sales racks and how stores set up the sales racks in the back of the store. Watch how the customer is attracted into the store for deals, and how they interact with sales racks with bright colors and limited time offers.

People watching in stores is fun, but what really excites me is creating successful sales pages online. And one of my favorite tools in creating increases in sales is the scarcity of a countdown timer. Combining a limited time offer with a countdown timer is possibly the best way to get a user to buy, because you are not only saying there is a limited time, but the timer is counting down. I build these timers and connect to my offers with two purposes: 1) I need to take an offer down because there are a limited number of seats available or we are launching a live training course at a certain date or 2) I am planning on raising the price of an offer and the countdown will be until the sale price is ending.

Either way, using the countdown timer on your sales pages is almost guaranteed to raise your conversion rates, if you learn how to execute the limited time offer properly.

PSYCHOLOGY OF SALES

The number one thing that is going to drive more sales for your business is to not make your website visitor think. Don't give them options. Instead, give them one option that you know they are going to want to take. Then through email marketing, you can offer a variety of other opportunities and offers they might be willing to take, while giving value and educating your buyer.

Here is something that I want you to do. Next time you are out shopping at a mall or any other retail store, watch the people while they are at the cash registers. Try to watch their faces while they are swiping their cards and purchasing items. Don't pay too much attention while they are walking around and picking out items, because that is not the exciting moment for the customer. The happiest moment most shoppers have in a retail store is just as they are swiping their credit card for payment.

It's crazy to think about, but people actually enjoy buying things! Your online experience can be just as exciting as the retail experience for your clients. That is totally up to how you position your sales copy and the excitement throughout your buying process. Flip your thinking upside-down and understand your customers are so excited to pay you, which equally you should be excited to get paid. Make your sales process a win-win where everyone is happy. Accomplish this and you are beginning to create raving fans for your business.

I have worked with hundreds of clients, and many of them believe that the sales process is not fun for the customer. That is just not the case! Add your personality into your sales process and your marketing, then you will see your audience and customers begin to identify with you, your marketing and your products. I have clients that have gone through my training systems, and they call and email me every once in a while to update me with the progress in their business. These messages from clients make my day, and keep me moving forward in creating more training and value for my clients. And equally, I try to make my training and other marketing fun, while also being helpful. Keep the sales process and fulfillment process fun, and your customers will continue to buy from you. This all begins with the words that you use in your marketing campaigns.

BAD COPY

With everything in life, there is the good and the bad. Often, the lack of sales and scaling a business can be due to bad copy. Don't worry if you think your copy is bad, know that you can get better! Know that we are not naturally given the gift of words, but know that we can learn how to communicate better. That is a fact! Where to start? Or how would you know if your copy is not good?

Start with knowing who your audience is and directing your text to communicate directly with your target audience. If you are not completely sure who you are writing for, then there is a strong possibility that you are missing the mark with your copy. Research your competition, and read how they are communicating with the audience, and that should give you some ideas. Once you understand your audience, learn what frustrates your audience and how they communicate with each other.

Next tip, every sentence you write should make a point and then end. Be careful of run-on sentences and thoughts. Be sure to make your point and then end your sentence. Be sure to structure your thoughts in an easy to follow pattern, and try not to skip around. In your mind, you might think that you are being super creative, when in fact you are just confusing your readers.

Grammar is very important, even if you are trying to create a statement with bad grammar, or if you are trying to connect with a different audience. Take my word for it, do not use bad grammar on purpose and think that you are creating a brand. I would say it is OK for one or two words to be branded in your logo or slogan, but continuing bad grammar through all your content can become annoying quickly. What is cute and creative can turn into a nuisance.

Tread lightly with your humor, as what is funny to one person is often not funny to the next. Unless you are a comedian, and that is why people are reading your content, it is probably best to steer clear of the overuse of humor in your content. Especially if you are trying to sell something that is not your latest comedy record. Yes, this can be contradicting as we have discussed in detail creating a brand, showing your personality and standing out of the crowd, but try to lean more on your personality and less on your jokes. Let your images tell the story and make them fun, but let your text have a certain degree of seriousness.

Do not alienate your audience with your copy, since your insults or comments can be misconstrued. People can take your content out of context very easily, especially when it is difficult to hear tone through your copy. Sarcasm and satire can be completely lost, and often can offend your customers in the process of purchasing. Just be mindful of others and potential sensitivities that people might have. I was listening to the radio the other day and heard some used car salesman pitching their offer, "our sign is outside and you would have to be blind to miss this deal."

And with that, I just realized that is the second or third time I have mentioned "used car salesmen" in this book, and perhaps that might offend you. Well, I am not that concerned because you are not my target audience. And if you are selling used cars, just don't be *that* guy

THE SEVEN PILLARS

PILLAR 7

CHAPTER 7

YOUR TEAM

Choose your team wisely, train them thoroughly and compensate your team handsomely. Take good care of your people and they will take good care of your business. Be sure to squash issues in your organization quickly and eliminate those with poor attitudes ASAP!

This formula works with two employees or 200 employees. Regardless of how many people work for you, or the organizational chart of how management handles departments, do not allow negativity in your workplace. Negative thoughts and actions can spread like wildfire, and before you know it, you will be firing entire departments of employees. I have seen this happen before.

Listen to your staff, have an open door policy, encourage new ideas and test their ideas to see if they work. Be sure to test their ideas, because there is nothing more frustrating than saying that you welcome ideas from anyone on your staff and then not executing some of the better ideas from them. Bottom line, be transparent with feedback and testing results from your staff's ideas. These activities can raise company moral and will encourage a more creative environment for your staff.

Give positive feedback, and when giving constructive criticism, whether to your staff, freelancer or contractor, always lead with the good points first. Put emphasis on the areas of their work that you truly are happy with and smile when you talk about the good work. Then when you need to communicate the poor performance, try to still keep an upbeat attitude to discuss. Remember to continue with the positive energy, even when you are delivering bad news.

Inspire your team to want to grow the business and increase sales by offering incentive programs, revenue share and possible bonuses for excellent sales performance. If your team believes they can improve their lives by helping your company grow, they will take extra special care as they work on their projects. These incentives can bring out the entrepreneurship mindset within your staff, as they become more invested in the business and sales of the product.

I can remember with my last employer, and I say last for two reasons: 1) the last company that paid me a full-time wage with benefits and 2) I will never work for another company again as a full-time employee. It was frustrating for the first two years, I had the ability to grow revenues for the company significantly and had presented to the owners on a few occasions. But when it came down to implementing my ideas, the owners were hesitant and treaded lightly on my big ideas. They eventually gave in years down the road.

As I kept pushing for my ideas, the company's CEO finally gave way and started executing more of my big expansion plans. After a few successful campaigns, we were adding to the bottom line and improving transparency with our customers. There were several occasions that I would have quit, and I had other job offers from companies throughout the years, but I stuck around to see where we could grow the business. My patience paid off in the end. Success!

Finally, I started receiving recognition in the office and was promoted to a new position that the CEO created to be his "right-hand man" or whatever that meant. He said, "When I get back from vacation, you will start reporting directly to me on all projects." I was excited to move out of my current position as creative director and into possible revenue share on the projects I was working on. When you are generating millions in revenue, sharing in wealth was an exciting offer for a broke 20-something-year-old.

Unfortunately, the CEO passed away while on vacation. True story! I can't make this up. I was really looking forward to expanding under the guidance of my mentor, and growing into a new position or potentially taking over new product development for a company where start-up capital was easy to come by. That was my end goal, having a seasoned entrepreneur who continued to fund my projects and I could continue to run tests for new product launches without needing to ever chase investor money again.

As an employee you should always keep pushing and eventually you will reach your goals and move up the company ladder. Then as a CEO, take good care of your employees and continue to let them grow into roles in your organization, and never forget that your employees are the most important value in your business. The company I worked for was sold, and most of the employees quit or were let go as the new company took over.

HIRING FREELANCERS

I have a love/hate relationship with hiring freelancers over the years, but I keep working with them because I need to find the best teams to handle tasks in their genius zone. If a team is good at HTML and CSS, I will not hire them to do graphics work for me. I definitely learned my lesson over the years to hire the people who are great at what they do, and then project manage the tasks as needed to complete diligently.

My biggest frustration in hiring freelancers is over-promising and under-delivering, or teams that cannot complete the work they promised they would complete. I swear, some people will say anything to land a project, and then make every excuse in the book on why it is not done. When you start hearing excuses, it might be time to start looking for a new team.

I have often joked about posting projects to freelancer networks, looking for a software developer with experience developing Death Stars in outer space. I am sure that a few offshore freelancers would have 10 years of experience with this development and will be able to complete the project in six weeks. It is funny to joke about, but when it comes to finding the right help to complete a project, truly the only way to test is by having them start on the first project. It is impossible to hire solely from "case studies" or from "portfolios of work" because freelancers often fabricate experience in order to get hired. It's sad but true.

The second biggest frustration is after the first successful project, sometimes freelancers can start slacking off or slow down their production. Don't get me wrong, it is great that freelancers work extra hard on the first project, but it is tough to manage timelines and deadlines if the work is getting completed slow-

87

er. Consistency is key and is tough to maintain, so often I look for teams who have worked with other clients over a long time period.

Communication is next on the list, as there really is no substitute for face-to-face time and being able to stand over someone's shoulder as they are working on a project. Technology has been great to allow us to connect and collaborate on projects with people from all over the world, but there is something to be said about the old school way of working. Personally, I am a huge fan of looking over shoulders, which can be the least favorite work method for many creative people or developers; however, to achieve the highest levels of productivity, I can quickly avert poorly designed or misinterpreted projects to pivot quicker. Often, I will have a freelance team working on a project overnight, as they work on the opposite side of the clock as I do, and when I awake in the morning, I expect to see a completed project. All too frequently, I start my morning checking over the work that was completed to find the concept of the project was completely missed.

If you can overcome the frustrations of working with an outsourced team, and they are able to work to deliver the quality of work you are expecting, on time, you found an awesome team. Treat your team well and continue to support their growth through your business. The key here is to find the right team of freelancers and treat them well, give positive feedback while maintaining excellent communication and hoping they will continue their level of performance throughout the projects. When you find the right freelance team, do not let them go. Retraining to your expectations can cause loss of productivity of weeks or even months while training a new team.

PROJECT MANAGERS

Although it depends on your business model, most companies will need to hire an excellent project manager before hiring other positions, like developers or sales people. When hiring a project manager, I look for someone who is loyal, honest and trustworthy. If this person is deceitful and they avoid deadlines, they will not make a good project manager. For my business, a good project manager is someone who will stick with me for a long time, as training new staff members can be very expensive.

I also look for a person who can wear different hats and is exceptional at a variety of tasks, but not an all-star at anything specific. Here is why I do not want my project manager to be an all-star or the best at anything: if my project manager is the best CSS person on my team, then all the difficult CSS projects could require his or her time. Therefore, the management of other tasks becomes a second priority when it should come first. You always want your project manager pushing along team members to complete work in a timely manner, and any distraction from that can delay projects.

The key role of management in your organization should be to work with staff members to remove the blocks that are holding them back from accomplishing their tasks as quickly as possible. By assigning too many projects to your project manager or any management staff, you can slow production and frustrate your staff. Your projects can become bottlenecked at one person, and this can be a disaster for productivity.

For example: the vice president of marketing at my former company wore so many different hats and was the point person for so many projects that the work that I needed to be reviewed would get pushed off. With these delays, my projects and timelines were missed, which made me look like I didn't reach my targeted goals and deadlines. Set up your team for success!

SALES TEAM

Sales and marketing are the core teams for most companies, and these teams need to be enthusiastic about your product. Keep your team motivated by using sales training techniques available through some of the best trainers like Dale Carnegie. Purchase books and share with your sales team, motivate your team to put a smile on their face and always keep reaching for their greatness.

But personal development and motivation will only go so far. The biggest failures of sales teams are due to poor education on the product and employees not fully embracing the company message. Educate your staff about your product and keep them embraced in the vision of your company. Good sales people are very hard to find, and it seems like the younger generation is not developing the skills like our parents and grandparents once had to build.

Call me an anti-millennial, but I have seen the younger generation is not willing to put in effort to achieve success through sales. You can blame society, their parents or the media, but regardless of whose fault, the old school "pound the pavement" sales people are retiring and eventually will be completely gone. This is even more of a reason to automate your sales process the best you can through leveraging technology.

The older generation consisted mostly of sales, customer service or blue-collar workers, and this new generation can get caught up in the activities that are not the foundation of a traditional work ethic. Don't get me wrong, I love the fact that I can make money while I am sleeping, but in no way does that make me lazy. Do I think a majority of the millennial generation are lazy? No. But I think there are far less "sales" minded millennials than previous generations.

CUSTOMER SERVICE

Customer service is the one department of a business that is most overlooked by CEOs. Either it is completely non-existent, the customer service team operates in a bubble away from the rest of the company, or they are well managed and on task!

If you have not taken any action on your customer service, now is a great time to get started. Be sure to look at your current reputation status by searching popular websites for reviews, and then begin scanning your social media accounts for bad comments. Keep a pulse on your customer service, as this is a great way to understand the negative pushback on your marketing efforts.

If your customer service team is operating in a bubble, this could be potentially a bad thing. All too often I have seen customer care employees poorly represent the company at the moment when the company needs to be represented correctly. You could invest hundreds of thousands, if not millions, of dollars in your business, and you do not want it all to come crashing down from a customer service rep who is having a bad day. Stay on top of your customer service and your reputation. It could cost you millions in sales if poorly managed.

Educate your customer service team on the best practices of the company and create responses for frequently asked questions. Automate as much of your customer support as possible leveraging technology, but then train your staff to pick up the human element to give that extra special care. If you balance your customer support and technology correctly, you should have the fewest employees creating the best customer care experience possible.

Another trick is to inform your customer service of new marketing campaigns. At times, the marketing or operations departments will not clearly communicate with the customer care department to inform on the latest marketing campaigns. In this case, you can create frustration inside the customer care team, and with the customers when the company is not communicating internally. This communication is best suited through management meetings and also through creating an internal communication system for the company.

Bottom line: when it comes down to your team, do your best to keep them happy and working hard for your company. Monitor their work output and quality of work. Be sure to award their successes and work together on improving their failures. Your team will take your company to the next level, so treat them well.

GRAPHIC DESIGNERS

For any company with an online presence, your graphic design team needs to be sharp and on-point with your company brand. Your graphics through social media, on your website and through your marketing will reflect your business to your potential customers; be sure that your message is clear and your branding is consistent.

Over the past 10 years, I have seen graphic design perfection and I have seen failure. And the failures do not fall on the designers; the fault is due to the lack of communication from the owner or visionary of the business. Graphic designers are not mind readers, and you will need to clearly communicate your message and your vision to the designer. This could take months or years to get the designer to the point they can operate without any directions from management.

You would be setting your business up for failure by consistently hiring and firing graphic designers, and there would be a greater chance that your brand identity will be all over the place. Keep your brand on point by hiring one great designer and keeping your designer happy in order to keep your brand identity consistent. Sure, you can find copycat designers who can mimic designs from other designers, but you would be far more productive keeping your core team busy and focused on the brand identity for your company.

For years I was overseeing a graphic design team, where our objectives were less focused on branding and more focused on direct response marketing. In this case, we could hire and fire designers based upon their performance. However, most companies do not have hundreds of millions of website visitors a week for testing design concepts, so this business was quite outside the norm. It was very nice having a large advertising budget to test theories and ideas, and what I learned from that experience was that ugly designs work. So funny to say, but for years we were trying to beat control banner ads, landing pages and emails that were ugly by design with our tests that were more pretty.

If you have a business where you can A/B test in a controlled environment, encourage your designers to test different ideas and designs to see what works in your business. Perhaps "ugly designs" work for your company as well! However, if you are unable to test, try to create graphics that are more aesthetically pleasing to the potential customers. Don't just say, "Matt says ugly works better. Let's go all-in on ugly!" Don't make any crazy adjustments to your business without thoroughly testing the concepts.

The creation of graphics for your social media should be a large focus for your ongoing marketing efforts. There are millions of companies who completely mismanage their social media accounts by not posting enough content. Have your graphics team busy working on tasks like email creation and other projects for your marketing, but remember that they can always work on tasks inside social media accounts. Create inspirational or other educational images that are posted every day. These posts will continue to grow the reach of your social media accounts and if done right, will elicit more comments, shares and engagement. Consistent posting should yield sales through social media channels as your social content is engaged by potential customers.

Take your social media accounts seriously, not just the paid traffic but the organic reach of your Facebook, Twitter, LinkedIn and other channels. When testing for organic reach, post 20 or 30 times consistently, then gauge the performance and pivot. All too often, companies fail by posting once or twice, then pivoting too early. Remember, this is organic reach and you do not need to 'pull the plug' too quickly. However, on paid traffic, don't wait to turn off failed campaigns.

Encourage your creative team to be creative. I know that sounds strange, but when the owner of the business is not creative, then the environment for the creative staff can be completely distracting to the creative process. During my years living in New York City, I have had the privilege of visiting dozens of offices of big companies that had creative departments, and I was fascinated by the offices that had social areas for games and other perks like refrigerators stocked with beers. After hours, the creative team would stick around the office and play a variety of games, sometimes talking about work but mostly just chatting about their interests. This was an eye-opening experience, considering at 5 p.m. every day, I was watching my creative staff clock out and leave for the day.

I tested this idea with my team and hooked up a Wii Nintendo, cracked open some beers and played Mario Kart with the team. I really believe that we increased the productivity throughout the day by increasing the employee morale. During the time we were playing games after hours, we continued to brainstorm ideas and come up with new creative designs for testing. I believe in a creative department that is unified, at least for a few minutes a week in non-work related activities.

WEB PROGRAMMERS

Equal to the graphic design team, your web programmers will have a similar personality, but at times they can speak a completely different language. I am a programmer, but I have been blessed with the ability to communicate with non-technologically minded people, as well as the developers of the world. But I am not your typical web programmer.

A typical web programmer will be someone who likes to focus on the work and work off of task lists. In my experience, many programmers have short fuses for those who are not technically minded, and they prefer to communicate with those who understand technology. There is nothing more frustrating than having to repeat yourself over and over until you are blue in the face from explaining programming. I understand that not every programmer is inpatient with layman, and if you find a patient programmer who is excellent at writing your website code, keep that programmer happy and employed with your firm; you found a rare find.

There are different programmers, front-end and back-end developers; and keep in mind, these programmers are good at what they know and be sure to keep them working in their genius zone. Don't ask your back-end programmer to design your website or work on your social media posts. You might look twice and find your programmer touching up their resume if you ask them to work on a project outside their expertise.

Great programmers are very difficult to find, mostly because all the best programmers are currently working on a project. At this moment, there are hundreds of thousands, if not millions, of great programmers buried in code and working to create the next big thing. After completing one project, they are often onto the next project. One of the biggest frustrations that programmers have is the complete lack of understanding on how much time programming actually takes. The perception of most non-technically minded company owners is that web programming is fast or cheap.

Yes, you can only pick two of the three, and this is my favorite graphic to show clients or non-technical minded people. Do you want the work done fast and cheap? Or good and fast? Which is your choice? Because we can adapt to your specific business needs just as long as you do not require all three.

Now here is where many business owners start getting into trouble with their programming: "we can just outsource the programming offshore." And with those words, you can almost guarantee a raise in your blood pressure and loss of sleep working with offshore development teams. Don't get me wrong, I have learned how and when to utilize offshore teams for development needs, but you have to be completely prepared to bring these outsourced teams onboard.

First, they will promise they can accomplish the project without completely looking over the code, and then they will show case studies from websites that they either did not program completely or the websites have nothing to do with the project you are starting. Once you find a team and you are confident they can get to work, now the problem is the communication as it seems like they speak the same language as you do at first, but as the project goes forward, you might reconsider their grasp of the language.

Next, the managing of expectations and the missing of deadlines and milestones is almost guaranteed. If you haven't gathered by now, I am speaking from years of experience. The quoted project delivery time is never accurate, and they seem to go missing for days at a time when you have a delivery date planned. If this sounds like something you want to experience, go for it! Hire a team offshore and get started working on a project. There is a 50/50 chance the project will be delivered and an additional 50/50 chance the project will be done correctly. And I think that is being fairly reasonable on those odds, at times it seems like a slim to no chance that project will be delivered as promised.

Let's go ahead and say that you found the perfect team or developer for your programming; be sure to keep them happy and around as long as you can. The turnover for graphic designers is not that bad, as the backups of all your company's work should be available. However, losing a programmer could be devastating to your company and a huge setback. Custom code is very difficult to navigate if the programmer is looking at the systems for the first time. This can cause your business to lose weeks or months as the new programmer is getting up to speed. Take good care of your developers, if that is in fact important in your business.

MANAGEMENT TEAM

Create a few all-star employees and form your management team. I really do believe that the managers need to be the best of the best in the organization, and people whom the rest of the staff will look up to. Not just because they are paid to, but that they admire and respect the management staff. I have seen solid management teams in action, and it truly is a beautiful sight to see. And equally, I have seen management teams that are killing companies slowly. It is a slow, painful death when the managers are the negativity and pessimism bringing down the ship.

Meet with your management team on a regular schedule and stay focused with the agendas. The management staff should be able to breakdown the successes and failures inside the organization rather quickly, and pinpoint the areas for improvement. The best management meetings consist of quickly running through what was accomplished, what was supposed to be accomplished and why the project was not completed in a timely manner; finally steps to solve the issues from a systems standpoint. If something is broken in the system, then fix what is broken. Again, if you are working on fixing the machine, then the system will run flawlessly. This way you will not consistently chase the issues, and you can proactively fix the problems before they start.

Make your superstar in your company the manager who oversees the most important aspects of your business. If your business is mostly sales, marketing or technology, make your manager that runs that department your superstar on the team. That person can be the point person on most of the larger projects that involve multiple departments, and your superstar can spearhead your massive growth projects. This way you have a team member who is on point and on call for any issues that arise in the project.

Bottom line is that a company is made up of all different personality types, backgrounds, experiences and people from different walks of life. If you are looking to expand your team, find the right candidates who fit the positions and try not to shove someone into a role where they have no business holding that role on the team. Use personality tests that you can find online to grade your staff members, and keep your good employees as long as you can, while weeding out the negative personalities and individuals who can hold you back.

CREATING A PRESENCE

CHAPTER 8

GROWING AN AUDIENCE

Your website is online and you feel good about your offers and call to actions throughout your site. All your follow-up emails are written and your graphics team has put together some compelling ads and landing pages. You feel good about your business, offers and product or service. You are ready to take your message to the world. But where do you start?

I first begin looking at what the competition is doing, trying to break down how they are marketing, using social media and growing their email list. Yes, I have a trained eye to know what to look for, but if you start now, you will find that you too can understand what your competitors are doing and what is working in their businesses.

As always, we like to get inspiration from our competition, and we are not trying to copy our competitors word for word. The best marketers learn this strategy to get inspiration or possibly reverse engineer sales funnels to understand how and why businesses run campaigns like they do. And you will need to find this ability inside you to take your business to the next level.

Or, perhaps you are stubborn, like I was for years with my business, and I refused to run campaigns mirroring my competitors. Take my word for it — I spent far too much of my own money testing my ideas when the how-to guides to success were right in front of me in the form of my competition. All I had to do was sign up to their email list, get their emails and buy their programs. Wow, I learned so much about my competition by purchasing their products.

All of this illuminated my path towards creating an online presence for my business.

The most important factor is creating a unique value for the marketplace and standing out with your best talents. Do not try to be everything to everyone, and understand that you will need to become the best at one thing, and stick with that. It has taken me years to understand what I am the best at, because historically I have just been decent at everything I do. I am a decent golfer, wakeboarder, surfer, guitar player, and so many other things that I just do decently well. But when it comes to business, decent often does not make the cut. People want to hire the best, and the being the best attracts attention online.

Often my competitors attract customers through flashy cars, houses, yachts and celebrity status. But I find all that flashiness to be a little over the top. To me, I want to attract new people with my message and not with my flashiness. So I wake up every morning and begin my process of combating mediocrity in my business by creating value and helping people in my organization to achieve their goals. My student's success through ScaleUP Academy is my Ferrari. I share my student's successes online to attract more students instead of sharing what car I drive. But to each his (or her) own.

Regardless of the attraction methods you choose online, find what works for you and stick with your messaging. Your consistency will attract new business to your products and services. The most important thing to remember is to convey that you are the best in your marketplace, and potential buyers should choose your business because... then give your best reasons. Deliver this message with your online presence and you will have a winning formula for creating success in your business. Be humble, give back to charity and above all, be yourself. Never create an online presence that is someone else, because your audience will eventually see right through your charade.

GRAPHICS

The first step to creating a strong online presence is branding your company with graphic design and making your brand consistent over all platforms. Understand that every social media profile is slightly different, with different size images to upload and specifications for images. Also, the call to action buttons are slightly different on each — for example: Facebook = Like Me, Twitter = Follow Me, YouTube = Subscribe, LinkedIn = Add Me. Master the graphics for your social media and your online presence is half way there.

In your graphics, be sure to include your main brand image, whether that is an image of you, your product or your logo. Then include a slogan or elevator pitch where a visitor can understand your purpose at a glance. I also like to consider adding a call to action right on the header graphics, such as: Free Workshop on Date. Don't Miss Out! If you do this correctly, you will have potential buyers signing up for your email lists without a single penny being spent in your advertising budget. And often users who find you through online channels, not through advertising, will be just as likely, if not more likely to buy than your visitors that are paid through advertising.

Create your graphics for the social profiles, tighten up and brand and stay consistent with your messaging. Once your graphic designer completes the branding project, get them to start working on your daily posting content. Yes, you will need to post educational or valuable content about your business every day. The secret here is to keep your community and audience engaged through daily content, and when I post to my page 20 times a day, I actually see a boost in engagement, sales and overall exposure. Stay consistent with your posting and stay on brand with your messaging. With this consistency, you will see an improvement in your advertising and organic reach of your social profiles.

Why? Because the more you post and educate your audience, the more engaged your audience will be. Also, the social media algorithms are mostly skewed towards those pages that post more regularly and have an engaged audience. You will need to find the sweet spot between just enough posting and too much and then execute. For your business, just enough could be three posts per platform per day, while too much could be 10 posts per platform. Remember, I am posting 20 times a day, but my page is all about Facebook marketing and showing entrepreneurs what I am doing to create success in my business. You will need to test to find what is working for your business. Note: start testing with a similar schedule as your top competitor.

ENGAGEMENT OFFLINE

The strongest social media plans begin with offline marketing. Crazy right? You would think that you start at 0 and begin online, but the strongest campaigns are also supported by your offline marketing. How is that possible?

For brick and mortar companies, leverage your foot traffic to engage online promotions. Do not let a single customer leave your establishment without signing up for your email list, or liking you on Facebook. Try to do this without being pushy. Add signage or include in your welcome message an offer such as, "Be sure to do [social media activity] and earn $5 your next purchase." Get creative and test new ideas, ask your customers what they would want and do your best to gauge what is working and what is not working. Stop activities on what doesn't work and attempt to scale what is working in your business.

If you do not have a physical location, that is OK. Utilize your business cards to drive a result, or create a print flyer for potential customers. Handouts with calls to actions are excellent for trade shows and networking events. Be sure to have something to hand out at these events, and never miss an opportunity to add a potential customer to an email list or social media profile.

The idea is to leverage offline advertising and engagement to drive your online advertising and engagement for your business. Let's face it, advertising can be expensive, so you need to leverage everything you can to try to ease the stress on your advertising budget. For some of my clients, they use their offline advertising and engagement to educate the potential buyers, then when the person sees ads online, they will be more likely to take action on the first impression. With that, lowering your cost per engagement when paying for impressions. But we will get into that more in the next chapter.

START WITH FB ADS

Whether you have one Facebook fan or one million, you should always look to grow your online presence on the social media platform with ads. Understand that you will not sell your product or service to every fan on your list, or on your email list, but you need to use Facebook systems to continue prospecting. Send your leads from Facebook to your website pages that explain your business and offer. Expand your reach with Facebook Like ads to introduce your business to potential buyers with a single click on the like button, and then over time you will have the opportunity to continue posting organically to your new followers on Facebook.

Remember to lead with value and education in your Facebook Ads, and always run campaigns to create more likes for your page. Seriously, always have like campaigns running. The "like" campaigns will help to search for additional interested prospective clients, so be sure to use your headline and graphics to explain the value for your potential clients to press the "like" button. You can run a various amount of ads in your like campaign tests, and just be sure to turn off campaigns that are not performing well. A good performance for a like campaign will be U.S. likes for under $.25 per like, and international English-speaking countries at under $.10 per like, with everyone else performing under $.05 per like. If your like campaigns are not performing at these numbers, continue testing new ads until you find the perfect ads for your business.

Then it is good to run ads to your fans and friends of fans with a very low or free offer they might be interested in. A low offer could be something for free, or a very low priced offer with a huge benefit. Again, test to find out what is working for your business and try to scale the successes and learn from the failures. The more interested the people are in your offers, the more likely they will be to sign up to your email list and take further action with your business.

Use retargeting ads through Facebook to give a secondary offer, if the first offer was looked at but not signed up for. Keep this window narrow, as you do not want to be wasting money after 10 days if they have not taken action with your offers yet. After the sign-up to the first offer, start advertising your next offer in the sequence, perhaps a free workshop or another action that you want the prospect to take.

Note: at this point it is a good idea to start qualifying leads with scorecards or questionnaires. You do not want to continue spending money in advertising and nurturing the lead if they are the wrong prospect for your business.

This is an excellent time to remind you that we have training on ScaleUP Academy where we show you exactly what is working right now in our business, and we have free workshops that you or your employees can attend online to learn how to master Facebook ads for your company.

CHOOSING WISELY

I always ask new clients, "Which social media platform do you want to be the best at?"

Often I hear the response, "All of them. I want to have more followers than my competition."

Although I love the ambition, but we need to find a place to start. And I recommend Facebook. Become the best at Facebook and all the other profiles can follow. This is not to say that you will not be posting anywhere else, no. Just focus your concentration mostly on Facebook to start, set up Facebook Ads for success and then move onto the next platform.

Why Facebook? Because Facebook has access to an extremely large audience and the ad network is very easy to master, once you know the expert secrets to mastering Facebook ads. You can find our strategies all at ScaleUP Academy. Also, Facebook is excellent for video, which can be a huge asset to your business in the future. If you are not currently leveraging video in your business, you need to get started ASAP. Video is an excellent way to educate, inspire and sell to your potential buyers. We have people finding our videos every day and buying products from us, and you can set up the same systems for you company too.

Some businesses can find massive success through Facebook and YouTube, while Twitter and LinkedIn seem to be working better in other industries. Regardless of your business, take a look at what your competition is doing and identify opportunities to prospect for new leads through each platform. Take massive action and test everything! Come up with new ideas and never rule out something just after testing once. Fact is, I have spent hundreds of thousands of dollars in advertising over the years, and I have learned what works and doesn't work. However, sometimes I am surprised when I would think something is guaranteed to perform well, but somehow it fails. After spending all this money, I am still just making educated guesses, and I am testing theories that I believe will work. You can do the same thing, and with time and experience, you will be able to become a master in advertising just like so many others across the world.

Or, you can choose to find an expert to hire to build your profiles and campaigns to the best of their abilities. The choice is yours, and the education to learn how to become an expert is a couple clicks away at ScaleUP Academy.

BE BOLD

The Internet is a noisy place, and it is so easy for anyone with an Internet connection to have a voice. This is fantastic for those of us who make money from advertising, as the more the merrier! But for those of us who are trying to stand out with our message, every new competitor is one step closer to taking the focus away from our businesses. This is a fantastic reason for you to start taking massive action in your business today! If you wait till tomorrow, you might have another 10 new competitors start up in your marketplace.

You need to stand out, be different and make your voice heard to resonate with your potential audience. But how? How do you stand out in the crowd? Rise above the noise? Be unique?

At this moment, you are reading a book that is my next attempt at standing out to be unique.

As I write these words, I have only slept a few short hours in the past two days, and I am trying to push forward to get this book completed in under 48 hours. Don't get me wrong, I love my sleep. Why torture myself? Because I have a plan to be bold and stand out.

I wrote the introduction for this book last year and have edited a few times. My book name and focus has changed three times over the past year as I have been talking to publishers. But I landed on deciding to self-publish. Why? First off, I do things because I want to prove to myself that I can accomplish big goals. Second, I didn't like any of the book offers for first-time authors.

The question is: "How am I going to get Forbes.com, Entrepreneur.com and other business publications to run articles on me?"

Note: here is where you should be brainstorming your message and how you plan to stand out.

I did some research and tried to brainstorm on ideas how to get their attention. I am 32 years old at the moment, so my age isn't an exciting headline. I'm an amazing web developer, SEO guy, marketer and overall business strategist doing a few million in sales a year through my clients, which is not very unique either.

In my personal quest to thwart mediocrity, I am continuing to stand out and do something that no one has done. Or at least, do something different that my competitors have not already done a thousand times. What am I to do?

That is when I decided to write a book in 48 hours. I tried to do it in 24 hours but I had a client who needed my attention on a project so my focus was taken away. Writing a book isn't the end of it. Now I need to get this book online for sale in the shortest time period and finally get the book onto the best seller list in weeks, not months.

My vision for the headline would go something like this: "College dropout goes from idea to best seller in 5 weeks." That timeline is not yet decided, per-haps I can do this in four weeks, but at the moment, I am still writing.

So what if my book does not become a best seller? Well, that is a risk I am willing to take. However, when you have a client with nearly one million fans on Facebook, a network of awesome friends in the industry and a few thousand dollars to invest in advertising, becoming a best seller is almost guaranteed.

Get started today: stand out and be bold. There are no excuses. Do it!

WHAT IS WORKING

Find out what is working today in social media. Everything online is changing so quickly and what is working today might not be working a year from now. This is another reason why we developed ScaleUP Academy, to show you ex-actly what is working today in building an online presence. We keep the train-ing up-to-date and you can choose to get notified with new training goes live on the site. We are dedicated to showing exactly what we do to create success in our businesses and keep you in the know.

It is crazy, but we learn new things every day too! We are the experts and we supposedly already know everything already, right? Wrong. In fact, I just learned something new over the past 48 hours. I will share with you here as an example, but note that the Facebook algorithms are constantly changing, and a year from now, this tip might no longer be applicable. But honestly, I think this will be a strategy for years to come.

I started my Facebook fan page a few years ago, but I got serious about promoting on my page in 2014. During the next year, I executed a successful product launch of our Search Engine Optimization strategies, which is still available on ScaleUP Academy today (but perhaps has been updated). During this product launch, I spent around $25,000 in 10 days of Facebook advertising. This ad spending shot up my engagement, likes and sign-ups to my course and I was able to make a profit. Success!

My thoughts were to just post on my page every so often while I was working on my next product for launch later in 2015. However, when I started to post more frequently later in the year, I was noticing that Facebook was not showing my messages to my fans. Note at this time I had over 80,000 fans on Facebook and when I posted to my page, less than 100 people were seeing my messages. This means that less than 100 people out of 80,000 were seeing anything I was posting.

I was furious. Why would I spend all this money getting people to like my page just to have Facebook's systems decide that my content was not good enough for my audience, or that my content was not desirable? So here there are dozens of experts saying to create content that is valuable and worth sharing, now I am spending hours creating this content and Facebook is not sharing with my audience. It's not like I was creating epic adventures and spending years of my life on creating the content, but what if I was, it didn't matter no one was seeing my posts. How do I fix this problem?

Earlier this week I start posting other entrepreneur's content to my Facebook wall, and viola - likes, comments and shares galore. Engagement is through the roof and I have grown my engagement times ten over the last 48 hours. Here I was for months, beating myself up about the poor engagement, thinking about ditching Facebook and moving to YouTube. But in a last ditch effort, I started posting other content that was already viral to my page, and my engagement is through the roof! That is the secret. You have to find relevant content that is already viral at the moment, meaning content that is being shared like crazy already through Facebook, then share that viral content on your wall.

Insanity! Now I have a new Facebook posting schedule, where I am scheduling 20 posts a day, and mixing in viral content that matches my message and peppering in my original content with the hopes that someone will click, like, share, comment and sign up to my offers. Keeping in mind, I am always running paid advertising and this organic reach tip has nothing to do with the advertising that is running that I am paying for. What I am mentioning here is my content that is not being boosted or paid for, and the content that is organically shared throughout Facebook. I want my posts to become viral, and get to the point that I no longer have to boost posts and my posts organically get shared throughout the entrepreneurial communities without my advertising dollars needed.

Your goal might not be to become the next influencer in social media and entrepreneurship, but that has been my dream for the past 10 years. If it is your dream too, keep working at it and eventually you will build a large presence online, just like I have. If your goal is to become the best in your industry, then this might also apply to you as well. My best advice is to stand out, get noticed and test everything. Find what works for your business and scale up! Educate yourself through ScaleUP Academy and leverage our expertise on what is working right now.

Consider writing a book and leveraging speaking engagement or events to establish yourself as being on the top of your industry. Learn from your competitors, buy their products and breakdown what they are doing well. Understand your customers, identify with their frustrations and solve their problems. If you are helping people, sharing your message with the world and trying to stand out with a great online presence, you should be able to make it in your business. Do not get discouraged and understand that there is always a new idea to test, track, pivot and repeat.

Do not give up, and know that you will always have the opportunity to be the next big success, just as long as you continue working at your business every day. If you quit, you fail. Guaranteed.

CHAPTER 9

SYSTEMATIZE

The key to building massive success is by taking massive action. However, if you are constantly doing busy work, copy and pasting, or building reports, you will never achieve your highest level of success, reach your goals or become wealthy. Doing busy work never gets you anywhere, and will only create busier work for you. Don't keep yourself busy; instead keep yourself productive building systems.

Once your systems are built and running, then you will focus your energy on tweaking the systems, rather than wasting your time and energy with busy work. Systematize everything you can in your business. If customer service is an issue, there is an app to make your customer service run smoothly. Set up the system and train your staff to run the operation, while keeping a pulse on the performance through reporting.

Create benchmarks for your system reports; for example: a customer service report will have the number of tickets created and closed in a day, and the average time to close a ticket. Watch these performance rates and train your staff to improve the numbers. Over time, you will go back to the reports to see how your customer service has improved. Without this system in place, your staff is merely responding to emails and verbally updating you on issues. Poor customer service protocols can set up your business for failure. Also, without having the proper benchmarks on your reports, you will have no basis for identifying the improvements of your systems.

Yes, there is an app for just about anything you need! To create a custom application for what your business needs, whether it is customer service, email marketing, CRM, reporting, etc., there is an app you can purchase for a small fee that can be up and running in minutes or hours. These applications are vital to moving quickly to create massive action. And if an application does not exist for your needs, you can find programmers to create these systems, if you desire.

Once you get familiar with the best applications on the market today, you will then be able to plan and execute marketing plans in hours, not weeks. This is why the entrepreneurs who create success once can duplicate that effort over and over again. Entrepreneurs who have already created success, myself included, can instantly point new business owners to an application that can be set up in minutes, and can change the future of a company. This is why my services are in high demand; however, I cannot work with every new client. With tens of thousands of names on my email list and hundreds of emails being received a day, I try to systematize the best I can to help as many people as I can.

Systems + Solutions + Demand + Massive Action = Massive Success

Without systems, I would not be able to communicate with thousands of people a day, and to expand my influence, I need more people just like you reading my words and hearing my voice through my videos and podcasts. The more videos watched and the more podcasts listened to, the more people will see my offers and choose to sign up or not.

I then use reporting to gather data on each step of my system to better understand how effective my offers are performing. Understanding what to look for is the key. I focus on what messages are shared, when and how those messages are engaged with, and then I check how those systems create dollars in sales. Perhaps an email was perfectly written and the offer was very good, but the email needed to be sent on a different day. Everything is worth a test!

SCIENTIFIC METHOD OF TESTING

If you told me in high school that I was going to become an author, I would have called you crazy. Keep in mind, I failed my ninth-grade English class.

Full disclosure: I actually passed the class for the year and failed the final exam essay. My parents went through a divorce that year. My attendance was less than par and the school had a rule that you had to pass the final if you missed 10 classes in a semester. My teacher failed me on purpose to make me repeat the class. She told me I should have showed up more frequently. Hats off to her and my guidance counselor for telling me that I would never amount to anything in life. Cheers!

In high school, I never would have ever thought that I would use scientific method in my life or algebra. But here I am, using scientific method for testing every day in my business, and patiently waiting for the day to use my algebra skills. For now, let me break down the scientific method for testing:

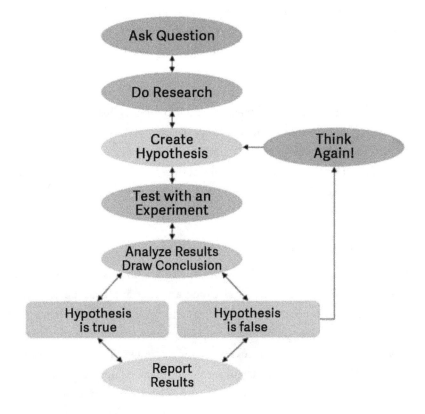

STEP 1: ASK A QUESTION

All too often we are not recognizing that we are executing this step in our scientific method, yet subconsciously we are asking a question. In marketing.

The questions can sound like, "How do I get more website traffic?" Or "how do I make more money?"

As business owners, we often ask ourselves and our staff these questions. How do we approach the question? What are the next steps? Our next actions can determine our future success.

STEP 2: DO RESEARCH

Here is where we need to jump into our competitor research to better understand how others are accomplishing their success. I believe that every great idea has been thought of and executed to some level, and we can leverage these genius ideas to propel our journey to success. Find someone who has done it before, faced the same questions in the past and created success.

STEP 3: CONSTRUCT A HYPOTHESIS

After our research, we then create a hypothesis. This is an educated guess based upon our research and can often take the form of an "if/then" statement. For example: "If I advertise this message on Facebook and target this audience, then I will generate more sales for my business." This is a very basic hypothesis, but for many of us, we have thought about running a Facebook Ads campaign that mirrors our competition.

STEP 4: TEST WITH AN EXPERIMENT

Assign a budget to test the hypothesis. This is where so many business owners make mistakes. Instead of assigning a budget and focusing on testing an idea, many entrepreneurs can abandon their plan to go in a different direction. The focus should be on making small, isolated tests where we eliminate as many variables from the test to focus on reading the results. Testing does not include rebranding a company, or spending too much time rebuilding an entire marketing plan. Also, do not fall into the trap of hiring freelancers to manage this entire process for you, as many freelancers can be good at Facebook Ads (for example), but they will not be focused on the big picture in what is being tested.

STEP 5: IS IT WORKING?

At this point you have an idea of how the test is performing. However, you have not completely analyzed the results. Perhaps the hypothesis or test needs to be tweaked, and in marketing this can mean a slightly different ad or landing page for the marketing experiment. It is also important to carefully consider the variables of the test, as these variables can show false readings when we get to the reporting of the test. Examples of variables in marketing could be: A/B testing landing pages and not controlling the source of the traffic. For example, some traffic could be coming from source X and other traffic from source Y, and if the traffic is seeing different ads on each source, then the conclusion of landing page X or Y working better might be influenced by variables in the experiment. Limit your variables and always have a control in your testing.

STEP 6: ANALYZE DATA AND DRAW CONCLUSIONS

The analysis of your data will be the cornerstone of your future growth in your business. Without understanding your data, future testing and hypothesis will be pointless. In campaigns that I have run throughout the years, we focus on watching for trends in the marketing reports, and our sole focus is to improve the systems to lower the cost per lead and raise the return on investment. Once you have systematized your marketing, drawing data and conclusions becomes a large part of your daily activities.

For example: I have previously built marketing machines for clients where we have 10 to 15 emails in a sequence to create sales. The front end of the machine attracts prospects and the emails turn the prospects into sales. The daily reports will show us both sides of the machine and allow us to create new hypothesis to test, such as: "If we send this email on day 1, then we will see an increase of 10% of sales in the first two days."

Then we set up the testing environment, eliminating our variables as best we can, and will watch the test traffic enter the system and read the reports on the testing setup. We were so good at testing that I would set up competitions with our staff to come up with the best emails to test. Whichever staff member created the best converting email would win a prize.

Keep in mind, every test that is set up needs to be statistically sound, meaning that you cannot set up a test with 10 site visitors. That will not work. I typically will not start testing until I have a control also, meaning that I will not test new landing pages until I find an ad that is working. I will not test new landing pages until I have a control ad (best performing). The idea here is to create a control landing page and a control ad. Your next step is to try to beat your best performing ad in a controlled testing environment. As for emails, I will not start testing new emails until I have a control and benchmarks for the ads and landing page, along with a control for the emails in the sequence. Understand the controls and variables in your scientific testing to create results that you can report with confidence.

CREATING WEB SYSTEMS

What is a web system? Is that just a website? Or is it a sales funnel? What exactly does this mean to systematize with web systems? The thought here is to leverage computer programming or other systems to eliminate the need for manual labor or copy and pasting.

The perfect example of a web system is one of the promotions that we executed for the launch of this book. Here is how the web system works in detail:

Goal: we want to sell this book through Amazon to build the rankings to become a best seller.

Note: every web system needs to have a clear goal and focus in mind.

Hypothesis: If I offer a free gift to those who purchase through Amazon, then I will create more sales and new loyal customers.

Problem: Amazon does not give me information on who buys for me to send free gifts, so I need to create a tracking solution for my customers.

The System: First I created a few ads about my book, and in these ads I highlight the benefits of why the potential customer might want to purchase the book. Also in the ad, I highlighted the bonuses of $197 in free training offered with the purchase of a book through Amazon. The clicks on the ad take the visitor to a landing page where I explain the offer in detail, include testimonials and reviews of the book for the potential buyer. Then I ask for the user to start the process by sharing their name and email.

I collect their name and email first, so if they are unable to complete the book purchase, I am able to remind the visitor about the offer. Similar systems have generated up to 70% of sales on day 1. The follow-up system will then convert 50% of the dropped off users over the next few days. If the system is not generating sales at over 50% of traffic in total, then I need to work on the email systems and continue testing until the numbers improve.

Here is where the magic happens. After the customer buys from Amazon, they will need to forward the receipt from Amazon to my web system. We have built these systems before where we are selling 3,000 to 5,000 units a month with an incentivized offer. Think about manually sending out 5,000 emails a month to users fulfilling their offer. It was an insane waste of time copy and pasting. Besides, by creating a system like this, we are virtually eliminating human error from the equation, and thus improving the probability of a positive customer care experience.

Now the web system is 'listening' for emails to arrive, and the system will read fields in the emailed receipt to verify that it was, in fact, a qualified buyer. If the system verifies the email, the system will then authorize sending access to the content. In order to avoid sharing or pirating the content, we have put systems in place to grant access using the email address and assigning a password to the user. Other systems in place are recognizing if the user is already on the list, or if the user is a new user, and then the system will make that determination to send the correct email accordingly.

Taking the system further, we programmed additional training workshops for the readers that they will receive over the next few weeks, since we know this customer is interested in taking their business to the next level. Through these offers, we are attempting to assist the customer in building their own systems and help expand their influence.

By creating this web system, we are able to serve an unlimited number of customers as our time has been eliminated from the equation, and thus we are infinitely scalable with the only constraints being our marketing reach. Therefore, we can leverage advertising to assist an infinite number of customers through our sequencing and potentially help an infinite number of entrepreneurs with their businesses.

PLANNING THE SYSTEM

The future success or failure for your system is in the planning. Understanding the technology and predicting what your audience will think and do. Predict what your audience is thinking through the marketing processes, and take extra special care through the customer care systems. Start planning at the end of the funnel or process, and then begin to work backwards. I find this planning procedure to work better than starting at the beginning and planning towards the end. Why? Because you can put yourself in the mindset of the end user, and think "what would I want to read or watch in order for me to take this next action?" Learn to use the eyes of your audience to predict their actions.

Words on these pages are meant to give you ideas on how to implement these systems into your business, and this book cannot give you the answers explicitly. You will need to interpret the messages into plans and action for your business. This is also why we have created ScaleUP Academy and the Million Dollar Plan workshops. Visit our websites and join our online training.

Digging a little deeper into this book launch plan, as mentioned in the last section, I can take you through the sequence of thoughts that brought me to creating this online system and the evolution of my business that has brought me to this point.

I have been building websites for over a decade, and in the beginning, website development was not as easy as it is today. In today's world, it seems that everyone has become an expert at website development or has taken a stab at creating their own beautiful website. I have no issues with this, because I love entrepreneurship and the fact that millions of people are starting their own businesses.

I wanted to compete with the other site builders in the marketplace, so I came up with the idea to beat the competition on price, offering $1 websites! My next thought was that I cannot live off of $1 per month, per site, nor can I afford to keep the business profitable. So I decided to upsell services in the systems. This was going very well for over the next few years; however, I came to the point that I realized that I do not like hosting thousands of websites for clients. Website hosting is not my passion, so I pivoted to higher level education, taking the websites from some traffic and some sales, to massive success and millions in sales. This is my passion.

To recap for a moment, I took a hard look at the end of the road and realized that website hosting was not my true passion in life. You should take something from this and apply to your business. If you are not truly passionate about the road ahead, change direction. Start moving towards your passions and future success, and envision yourself at the end of the road. If you can envision your future success, and what your day-to-day will look like, then you seem to be on the right path and you need to continue forward.

I began creating my online training systems, ScaleUP Academy, and on the first training launch, my Advance Search Engine Optimization Course, we had hundreds of students go through and amazing success stories. We are off and running in the online training space! This has always been a goal of mine, ever since I started watching Internet marketing training content back in 2004. I was extremely excited, and this excitement has carried me through creating hours of training videos and materials.

However, something was still missing. I began my journey at the end of the road, and I am slowly working backwards towards my lead magnets and main offers. But the offer of ScaleUP Academy is not a sweet enough offer to me. I want to give more value. The thought processes continued on for months where I finally came to the conclusion that the best knowledge I have to offer is building these systems to take businesses from six figures a year up to seven figures a year in revenue. The strategies, planning and execution of these plans is my objective, and I need to create a solution that could help thousands of entrepreneurs.

It was this point in my plan that I decided that I needed to write this book, and create additional value and education to accompany the book online. At this point, I have a middle range product which is ScaleUP Academy, a 12-module training course along with the advanced mastering courses, and I have a book concept, which will be at the beginning of my funnel. I started researching my competition, and what other experts are doing online and here is where I came to with the planning on my product line: start with the book, free training, free workshop, paid group coaching program, ScaleUP Academy and finally my inner circle for clients.

These programs start with the book, which is an excellent tool in my marketing promotions, and then I can attract new prospects with my free training and workshop offers. If the prospect likes the training, I can offer a group coaching level of training as the next product. I like the group coaching model for the Million Dollar Plan because I can give awesome value during our live workshops, then answer questions at the end of each workshop. The fact is, there are millions of entrepreneurs online trying to compete for the same market space, and it doesn't matter how great their ads are or how beautiful their logo is, they will need a big idea to take them to the next level. The Million Dollar Plan coaching program helps business owners with creating their breakthrough ideas.

Going beyond the coaching program, students can also learn exactly how we create our results online. We show them step by step in our ScaleUP Academy training. They watch onscreen as we create sales funnels, website traffic and make sales. This is truly the next step as once you have your big idea, it is time to test! And we show you step by step how to test your concepts in your marketplace. Lastly, we offer our services for clients who decide to hire our team to build the systems. A solution for every budget.

OK, now we have our plan and our spectrum of solutions, and we can start planning out the system and predicting the audience's actions. Now understand that this flow and the thought of educating your customer might not be the solution for every business, but you would be surprised how your sales can improve through educating your prospect before asking your prospect to buy.

BUILDING YOUR PLAN

The psychology of my sales process begins with being disruptive in a noisy marketplace. Without the disruption, I am unable to create clicks and sign-ups. Here is where you need to start getting creative. What do I mean by creative? Do you remember the "Congratulations You Won!" website banners from years ago? Those banners disrupted hundreds of millions of people worldwide, and I designed many of these banners in my earlier years. We could not beat that promotion, and we signed up millions of users to the offers. This is an extreme example of being disruptive, and I have dialed down my marketing ridiculousness, but sometimes you just have to test everything to see what works.

If you cannot get past the idea that I created banners that might have frustrated you, keep in mind that I created banners that were ripped off by people who then put a voiceover on the banners. My banners were pretty obnoxious and flashy, but were not the banners with the spoken voice. Mentioning these promotions that I ran for my client years ago was not meant to frustrate you. The purpose was to explain what disruptive means. And if you are still frustrated with those banners that stopped running years ago, then these banners really disrupted your lives. Think about that for a moment, is your advertising that disruptive? Are you making an impact with your messaging and your business?

Going back to the thought process of the visitor, they have now clicked on a promotion and arrived at your landing page. Here is where the magic begins in the mind of your visitor. Your page needs to clearly communicate the following: 1) trust 2) who this offer is for and 3) can the visitor get results from this? If your website visitor is on a trustworthy page, often this page should match the ad that is clicked on, and if they believe that this product or service is for them and they can get the desired results that they are looking for, a percentage of your visitors will take action.

Keep in mind that a percentage of your traffic will leave this page and never view anything from you again, so be sure to put your best foot forward here. The idea is to get these visitors to sign up to your email list, where you can continue to give value and educate on the sale. Education of the sale can be case studies, news articles and publications or helping the prospect to understand that this is the right product for them. And you have to do this using technology to the best of your abilities. Again, you cannot get on the phone with every person and try to educate and sell over the phone. If you are starting a call center, you will need to educate your staff on how to sell over the phone. Either way, leverage technology to create sales processes that educate and seed the sale.

Focus on giving value and continue to give value. Leave the prospect feeling as if they have been given a gift and that they are happy to have found your business. The Internet is a noisy place and we have to stand out with our advertising. Once the prospect has signed up to our list, we have to give value and nurture the prospect through the process of turning into a customer. There are a variety of tactics that are currently working, but the key is to give the best value that you can offer, without expensing too much of your time in the process. Remember, your time is the most valuable commodity that you have, and we cannot buy more of it. Spend your time wisely, and leverage your systems to educate your buyers and give value.

ADVERTISE

We have reached chapter 10 of the book, and up until this point we have largely been planning and building for future success. What would you say if I told you that so many entrepreneurs try to jump to this section, without going through all the steps that we have discussed in previous chapters? Sure, if you can master the setup of Facebook or Google ads, you can create wealth in your business. However, it is very important to have the right plan, set up the proper web systems and create a scientific testing process for your advertising.

Advertising is an excellent way to waste money, if you do not take the correct steps before moving into the advertising phase. Equally, even if you went through all the steps, setting up advertising campaigns incorrectly can leave you spending your entire ad budget in a single day.

In my 10+ years of advertising and marketing, the number one thing that I hear from existing business owners is, "we don't use ___fill in the blank ad method___ because we tested that before and it didn't work." Don't let this mindset hold you back from massive success.

Think about it this way — have you tested every possible ad, with every possible ad target and every possible landing page to try to find what works for your product and industry? Have you exhausted every possible scenario, looking for the best way to create results through the marketplace for your business? Is the answer no? Then you have not tested everything!

For years I worked with a client who was so stubborn and would not test new things. He used to say, "I refuse to test TV ads because we tried that and it didn't work." Years later I finally dug up that TV ad they tested and it was horrible. The brand was completely lost, there was no call to action, no incentive to take action and the message was not clear at all. What if I would have tested a TV ad and we saw 10 times growth in sales? What if? Instead the client said, "people do not remember what they had for breakfast, let alone what they saw on TV."

What is the logic in that? If your top competitor is advertising on TV, wouldn't you ask yourself why? Why is my competitor doing better and selling more than my business? What can I do with my advertising to improve my results? How can I borrow ideas from their success to generate my success?

If you have been in business for a while, then perhaps there are instances where you have a bad taste left in your mouth from a previous campaign. This reminds me of another situation, which is really funny because the issue came back around, twice.

Let me explain: I was playing golf in a charity tournament a few years ago, and one of my golf teammates asked what I do for a living. I briefly explained that I do web development and marketing. Well, he instantly jumped into pitching his idea to me. This is something that happens all too often. After his pitch, he asks my advice on how I would advertise this startup, and considering that his business is a service that people are searching for on Google, I instantly come to the conclusion that Google is a great place to start advertising.

However, he goes on to explain how his previous marketing guy set up Google ads and accidentally did not set a low budget. After the marketing guy set up the ads in Google, the owner woke up the next morning to see thousands of dollars paid to Google for advertising because the budget was not set low to start. He told me that he fired the web guy, turned off Google ads and will never try Google again.

After listening to his story, I responded with, "That is tragic, and I am sorry to hear that. Perhaps we can connect later to come up with a new strategy." Then after a few follow-ups, which he never followed up with, I gave up trying to help him. Figured that he moved on and this project was no longer a priority.

Fast forward 10 months and I had a lead come in from a referral. "Let me send over this guy's information. He is trying to start up a new business and is having issues finding an expert like you to help out. I will send over his contact information." Here comes an email from a familiar name, pitching a similar business that I vaguely remembered. His email started by saying, "You come highly recommended by several people in the community, so I had to connect with you." I couldn't pass up this opportunity to follow up on progress.

We get on the phone to discuss and he remembers me after a few minutes. Refers to me as the 'Google guy' and says that he will not advertise again on Google. I never heard back from him. Of course, I followed up a few times trying my best to help. But it is crazy to think that someone who had a bad experience with someone setting up ads incorrectly can hold back a business for success in the future. The moral of the story is to let go of your past experiences and understand that one bad test does not mean that traffic source is ineffective for your business.

I have no idea what happened to this guy's business, but I truly hope that he was able to let go of the past and start advertising on Google again. But he needs to find an expert who cares about his money as much as he cares. Google ads can work, if you know what you are doing.

GOOGLE ADS

Leveraging Google AdWords can help you reach 90% of Internet users worldwide. Google allows us to target users based upon what they are searching for through the search network, along with their interests and trends through the display network. Google also has access to YouTube advertising and advertising through mobile applications that could be sold through iTunes or Android app stores.

The numbers are staggering on how many people you can potentially reach through Google Ads, and you can get started today by setting up a free Google AdWords account. With most clients, I recommend starting with testing the Google search network first and then moving onto testing the Google Display Network, retargeting campaigns and YouTube ads. There is so much opportunity and I could honestly write an entire book just on advertising through Google.

Are Google Ads going to work for your business? My answer is make them work! Figure out what your competition is doing and try to set up your ads in a similar way. There are several software programs that you can use to spy on your competitor's ads. This will allow you to create a similar ad campaign with the hopes of converting some of those potential customers to your business. This could carve out a piece of your marketplace and support growing your company. Keep testing ads and find what works for your business.

There is not a 'one-size fits all' marketing strategy for Google, so definitely do your research and plan new ideas to test. However, the most important advice I can give in this book is to read the Google AdWords Terms of Use and Advertising Policies in detail. Google AdWords is very particular on who, what and how you can advertise on Google AdWords, so be sure that you are not in violation of their terms. Violating their terms can get your URL permanently blocked from their system.

BONUS: When you get ads performing well on Google, Bing has a service to migrate your Google Ad campaigns to Bing. Even though Bing has a much smaller reach, it is still beneficial to bring your ad campaigns over to leverage on the Bing network. It also doesn't take much time to set up the same ad campaigns.

FACEBOOK ADS

Google has been the 500-pound gorilla for years, but Facebook has been improving their ad systems and have quickly risen to one of the top advertising platforms online. Through Facebook Ads, you are able to reach customers based upon interests and by the information users fill out in their profiles. This is valuable as Facebook has leveraged people's information to create a network of interest-based targeting where you can even target income and net worth of individuals through the Facebook network.

Facebook Ads can reach customers through a variety of campaigns, all managed within the Facebook Ads platform. Campaigns can be set up to generate more 'likes' on your fan page, views on videos, clicks to website and also conversions throughout your web systems by using pixels. Mapping out your Facebook Ad campaign can go hand-in-hand with your marketing strategy through email and creating different levels of offers through your sales funnel process. Additionally, Facebook can also target users on Instagram.

Leveraging Facebook and Google properly can run your entire marketing strategy and help you reach billions of users worldwide. It's hard to imagine two networks can help you reach almost everyone on the planet who has an Internet connection. Meanwhile, both of these companies are working diligently to bring the Internet to more people around the world, thus adding to their networks and reach worldwide.

AFFILIATE MARKETING

Facebook and Google's ad platforms are largely based upon a CPC (cost per click) bidding strategy where business owners can bid for clicks based upon a variety of variables in the algorithm including relevance, competition and bid price. However, there are other ways to advertise your business and one of these other means of advertising is called affiliate marketing.

Affiliate marketing is a performance-based advertising model where business owners can advertise their offers through other website owner's networks. Through the affiliate marketing strategies, deals can be struck to pay commissions for sales or leads into a sales funnel. Often affiliate campaigns will not include any exchange of money for impressions or clicks, only when a sale or sign-up occurs for the advertiser. This is where affiliate marketing differs significantly from Facebook or Google pay per click advertising.

Breaking into affiliate marketing campaigns can be difficult. In fact, it can be nearly impossible for some. The best affiliate marketers and marketing platforms keep their systems locked up and rarely allow new advertisers into the mix. Why? Because the space is limited, and if a new advertiser does not have a proven sales funnel or track record, it creates a risk to the integrity of these platforms and networks.

On the other hand, there are a few larger networks that are more open to allowing new members to join, and also will let rookie advertisers into the network. However, many of these networks encourage you to advertise your own

affiliate campaign to your own network. This means you can ask your customers to share your affiliate links to your products to their friends and family and opens the door two ways: 1) allowing you to incentivize your customers to share your products and services and 2) allowing you to create statistics on your affiliate campaigns to share with other affiliate networks to expand beyond your network reach.

Setting up an affiliate marketing campaign relies on excellent reporting and setting up systems to automate tracking for affiliates, with accounting and paying out accordingly. There are companies that have affiliate marketing strategies that are signing up thousands of new members a day and selling thousands of products without having to pay a single penny out of pocket. This is the beauty of affiliate marketing. You only pay when you make money and share the revenue with the person who referred the sale.

One of the best places to get involved in affiliate marketing is by going to specialized conferences and meeting other affiliates face-to-face. Or at least that is where many of my clients have built their networks and grown their advertising reach by connecting with potential advertisers at conferences. The Internet and social media is awesome for connecting with people, but nothing beats meeting someone in person.

OTHER AD NETWORKS

There are a thousand different ways to advertise your business, both online and off. Many of the ad networks are through social media companies like Twitter, LinkedIn, Pinterest, Stumbled Upon, etc. In fact, every year several new companies are launched and have different ways to connect with your potential audience. However, I highlighted in this chapter my three favorite ways to market a business online. Perhaps you find success in LinkedIn ads or Twitter ads, which is awesome! Test everything to find what works!

The key to marketing success is to go where your customers are. Learn about your customers, their frustrations and what they want. Carefully craft your marketing message to deliver the pain and pleasure, solving their problems with your product or service. Test everything you can, understand how to test using scientific method approach to testing and have reporting set up to gauge the results of your testing efforts. Test, pivot, retest and repeat. Never stop testing new ideas.

MAKE YOUR ADS STAND OUT

I can't tell you in this book exactly what ad is going to work for your business. But I can tell you to try different ads and get creative. If everyone is testing a message like, "Learn how to set up Facebook Ads," then maybe you should have your ad copy differ to stand out. Here is an example idea, "Facebook ad headline that generated a 400% increase in clicks." Perhaps that is not your focus, but see how different that title is, and I guarantee that title will get far more clicks than the first title.

Make your images stand out by using bright colors that differ from the rest of the page. Use calls to action and have a very clear offer for your potential customer. Give value and be sincere. Do not trick your visitor or frustrate them. You have one chance to make a good first impression, and often the best first impression is education. Educate your potential customer on what your business is, how your product helps create a solution and who your product is for. If you set up the right targeting in the ad campaign, hopefully you reached the best audience for your product.

If you have not reached your desired results, go back to the drawing board to create a new ad test. When you are looking through your reports, find what is working and attempt to identify what is not working. Eliminate the elements you believe are causing the test to fail and retest with your hypothesis.

Continue testing, retesting and pivoting until you find exactly what works as you are able to start drawing conclusions. Going forward, continue to test new ad platforms and expand your reach by becoming an early adopter of new technology. The world is moving fast, and if you are always playing catch-up, then you might miss out on opportunity.

Go towards new opportunities and stay open to change. Always test new ideas and watch how your reports will change over time. Identify hours of the day, days of the week and special days in the year that perform better than others. Focus on building a team around your advertising efforts and understand one person cannot manage an entire million-dollar business. If you have a single person managing your entire ad strategy, you are missing out on opportunities and leaving money on the table.

Expand your campaigns, budget, reach and marketing team. Pay your team well and invest into their future education for success. Attend workshops and conferences, network and make new friends. Do not operate inside a bubble. Share your results with others and become part of mastermind groups to learn what others are doing to create success. There is an infinite opportunity for you to grow, and it is up to you on how far you are willing to go to reach your full potential.

TECHNOLOGY MANAGING ADS

Leverage advertising applications that track, report and help optimize your ads across multiple networks. This can save you hours in your workweek and thousands of dollars in your advertising campaigns. There are dozens of these applications, so be sure to find the best technology that suits your needs.

Typically, I do not jump right into these software solutions right away. I will use the native ad platforms, like Google AdWords and Facebook Ads first, and then as my ad spend grows to over $1,000 a day or so, then I will look into the best solutions to fit my needs. I believe one of the issues today is entrepreneurs get the shiny new object syndrome. This is where a new technology would come out, and through social media it seems to be the talk of the town, yet the solution does not necessarily fit your needs.

Stay focused on your business, and stay focused on the majority of your business. If Twitter ads are driving less than 5% of your sales, for example, do not focus too much of your time on those ads. Focus a majority of your attention on the ads that are performing the best, and slowly continue to tweak or phase out your advertising that is not performing for your business. But test everything! Track your testing performance leveraging technology and continue to pivot until you find what is working for your business.

In all of my years in marketing, the first ads typically do not meet my expectations. Why? Well, I have very high expectations. Set your goals for your advertising campaigns high, and keep tweaking until you reach your goals. If your systems and sales funnels are flawed, tweak your funnels and continue to come up with new creative ideas on how you can create massive results.

CHAPTER 11

REPORTING

G et serious about your reporting. Every great CEO understands the reports for their business - whether it is a marketing report, customer service, productivity, fulfillment or sales. Take the time each day, week or month to analyze the reports that you need to keep the pulse of your business. Without understanding your reports, you will be leaving keys to your company to someone else, or perhaps no one will be watching the reports.

You would not believe how many business owners are completely lost when it comes to their reports on their website traffic. I encourage every client and everyone reading this to stay up-to-date with your advertising reports, understanding where your dollars are going and what your ad dollars are producing for your business. Try to identify where the leaks are in your systems, and plug them with testing and new solutions. Without knowing the data inside these reports, you will not be able to identify trends to create new testing ideas.

Go beyond the surface of the report to understand what the numbers mean and analyze each line item with scrutiny. If you do not understand part of your report, ask someone on your team who should know to explain for you. If they are unable to explain, find out why and possibly look to find someone else who can better set up your business reporting. Encourage your team to keep up with education on new strategies and technologies. Online advertising and reporting is changing constantly, and you need to keep your team up to speed on the latest trends in the marketplace and within your industry.

Work to automate your reports the best you can, breaking down the reports into different levels where you can identify trends in your business. Try to match up these trends with other reports, for example: point out when new marketing campaigns are launched and cross reference in your customer service report to see if there is an increase in tickets opened. Same goes for fulfillment issues and other areas of concern in your business that you can cross reference with customer service reports.

The only way that you can grow a company and scale with sustainability is to systematize your reporting to understand how to maximize your return of investment. If/when you get to the level of spending $1 million a month in advertising for your business, a 1% increase in your return on investment can make a huge impact in your bottom line. Identifying the smallest numbers in a report can yield thousands of dollars in profit saved for your business.

Previous companies I have worked with had a handful of analysts going through reports all day, looking for areas of concern and places to improve. They would report back to the CEO on their findings and spend their entire day looking for issues and trends. The CEO would then confirm the trend through cross analyzing and call up the marketing team to create solutions. The marketing team would test an idea to fix the problem and then analyze again. For massive marketing companies, these small changes in the marketing campaigns can make a huge difference in profits.

During my years spending more than $1 million a month in advertising, I have been able to identify large gaps in reports that over time have yielded hundreds of thousands in recouped revenue. In fact, a former client's CEO said on several occasions, "If it wasn't for Matt, we would not be in business right now."

I am not an amazing analyst. In fact, I am terrible at Excel. I have no idea how to set up a pivot table, nor how to merge fields or set up functions. Yet I was able to learn how to read reports and come up with a hypothesis using scientific method for testing ideas. The secret is to identify a trend, find an opportunity for improvement, create a strategy and execute. Then I would identify what I think will happen in the report and watch to see how it improves the numbers. If the numbers do not improve, then I test again and again.

GOOGLE ANALYTICS

Google Analytics is free to set up on your website and is a wonderful tool. Study it and know how to set it up properly. The proper settings for Google Analytics include leveraging the conversion pixels and goal tracking inside the program. This can include lead, add to cart, sales and eCommerce tracking for the cost for sales. When all this is set up properly, you are able to visually see where traffic, leads and sales are coming from.

You can also set up your sales funnel to be tracked through Google Analytics. This means you can identify the original source of a lead and track all the way through your email and social media processes to see where the lead comes back to your site and eventually the medium that creates the sale for your website.

Integrate your Google Analytics into all your web properties, including systems you might use like ClickFunnels or other software such as appointment scheduling, etc. Your Google Analytics account can break down your website traffic, showing where leads come from and fall off on your sales process. Understanding the traffic and performance is the first step to improving your sales and performance.

Google Analytics is mostly a counting system, and does not necessarily identify who the user is. It just knows how many users there are. To take your reporting deeper, you will need to integrate a customer relationship management (CRM) system to understand who the visitor is and what they are doing on your website.

INFUSIONSOFT

To better understand who is doing what on your website, I leverage Infusionsoft. This powerful tool helps me understand who signs up, opens email, clicks on emails, buys products, visits my website and takes action with my offers. Leveraging Infusionsoft and the reports that come with the software, I am able to create a dashboard that gives me a pulse on my marketing efforts at a glance.

Also, Infusionsoft has powerful application program interface (API) plugins and other tools that can be created custom by their marketplace partners. It is definitely a powerful tool if used correctly. So many Infusionsoft users are not fully leveraging its power as a reporting tool and marketing automation system. For example: not only can the system send you an automated report on users who have taken actions on your site, but you can also set up the system to send marketing offers based upon different actions taken within your application. For instance, if a user reaches a certain lead score, based upon your set scoring algorithm, that user can be moved into a new action set that sends emails with special offers.

In short, Infusionsoft is not only a CRM and marketing tool, but the system can automatically send emails and offers to your customers at the perfect time, based off their actions. Infusionsoft is not the only software platform that does this, but it is the software solution that I will use going forward, as explained in previous chapters. This system is so widely integrated into every aspect of my business and can create reports on virtually any breakdown of who is doing what on my website.

OTHER REPORTS

There are dozens of software systems that offer reporting, and it is up to you to find the reporting systems that work best for you. When you look for software solutions, such as customer service, fulfillment, project management and other systems that you might implement into your company procedures, be sure to pick a solution that has excellent reporting. Better yet, choose systems that integrate into your CRM platform. If you choose Infusionsoft as your CRM, be sure to see if the other systems have integration for Infusionsoft.

If an API is not available, consider creating a custom API or looking for a different solution. I always find what I am looking for if I look around a bit, and the people in the Infusionsoft communities are very helpful to find solutions as well. Not to mention, we have communities for ScaleUP Academy that you can reach out to find solutions from our experienced members.

CHAPTER 12

SCALING

A s owner of ScaleUP Academy, ScaleUP Media, ScaleUP 360 and ScaleUP Consulting, you can instantly see the word that I like to use the most. SCALE! Scaling is the name of the game because it is easy to sell your time and not so ease to scale your time. Our time is the number one most valuable commodity that we have because we only have so much of it. Currently, we are not able to expand our time or manipulate it. I hope to live longer than the previous generation, but so far, there has not been any guarantees on the expansion of life spans indefinitely. Therefore, time is the most valuable resource we have, so use it wisely.

Scaling a business means different things to different people, and to me it means to create a business that can actually grow. So many business models are not scalable, or at least scalable while maintaining integrity and sustainability. In a sense, you might have to reinvent your business slightly in order to find a new scalable solution. For example: I am unable to consult for 1,000 clients with one-on-one time. However, 1,000 clients can easily watch videos from me and join my live webinars to ask questions with the group.

Perhaps this is not your business model, but you have to think outside the box to consider how you can create a solution to scale your products or services. With scaling your business comes a host of different problems. Think of every problem you run into now with your business, multiply those issues by 10. This is why it is so important to set up your systems before scaling and set up your systems from the beginning with scaling your business in mind.

135

Be careful when setting up your systems to understand the setup's structure for growth and expansion. The worst thing to do when scaling a business is have to backtrack to set up a system over again because it wasn't done right the first time. If you are expanding into other languages, take that into consideration from the beginning. Set up your website for simple expansion to support other languages. And no, language plugins for translation are not a solution. You have to employ real translators and set up your websites correctly.

Be sure that your marketing campaigns, sales funnels and automation are all set up with expansion in mind. When I am setting up a business, we are always very clear on the expansion ideas from the beginning, because that completely changes the way I would program or organize a web system for future expansion. This is also another reason why to hire the right people from day 1, instead of trying to cut corners with a team that will not be able to grow with your organization.

Perhaps the best piece of advice I can give you is to hire someone to help consult for your business who is an expert at how to scale or can build a company that can scale. If, in fact, you are interested in growing an online "empire" or large organization, choose to learn from those who have already done this before. Note: you are reading a book at this very moment, written by someone who has grown massive organizations and created massive results for clients.

Choose the architecture and framework for your website and web systems that can grow to scale, and understand the limitations of the software that you need to use to get started. The limitations in the software you select can also create a road map for future growth that needs to happen in your business structure.

For example: I recommend WordPress, hosted on your servers, as the website framework for almost every business getting started, except for SaaS (software as a service) businesses. If your company is planning to grow beyond 100,000 members, perhaps a different website architecture might be needed later down the road. But WordPress could manage your growth up until a boiling point when a new solution will be needed. However, that solution could be years down the road. This is just one simple example and you should consult a trusted development team for getting a better road map.

I believe in building on a limited budget, then continuing to reinvest into the systems as the organization grows. Perhaps this is from years of pitching investors and basically begging for money, something I will never do again. Once you build results, continue investing in your systems to make them better, expand your advertising and grow your network and reach. Your success will attract success into your business. If you are an investor and really liked this book, drop me a message online and I will introduce you to projects we have in the queue currently. Yes, I am always working on the next big thing, and always interested to connect with those who are also working on big things.

Keep your goals high, but stay humble along the way. This is something that I learned in my years working with musicians, as they would go on stage to thousands of screaming fans and give the performance everything they have. And then would come off stage and be so humble. Not that every band was like this, there are definitely those who are not appreciative, but the celebrities and musicians who have influenced me throughout the years are those who are massively successful, yet extremely down-to-Earth and humble.

Leverage your web systems and advertising to expand your influence and reach new potential customers. When the stars align, everything is clicking with your web systems and advertising. Each piece is calibrated and tweaked, and the sky is the limit for your business. Stay focused, maintain your integrity, create solutions that help people and always help those who are less fortunate by giving back.

Believe in yourself, your team and in your dreams. Push yourself to reach for higher goals and never stop learning new things.

THE NEXT STEP

Thank you from the bottom of my heart for reading my first book, the Million Dollar Plan. My objective in life is to help entrepreneurs on their path to success and help those less fortunate. In purchasing this book, a portion of the book sale has been donated to charity. Read more on my website.

If you haven't signed up already, we have a free workshop to help you take the next step. Visit http://milliondollarplan.net to learn more about the free workshop and sign up.

The next step is yours. Take all this knowledge and get started applying these strategies to your business. Remember, we have a group coaching program that has limited space, so be sure to visit http://milliondollarplan.net to learn more. We also have ScaleUP Academy, where we show you the up-to-date strategies that are working in our business today, and exactly how to execute in your business. Lastly, if you are ready to take a big step forward for your business, inquire online about the availability of our one-on-one consulting services.

Space is limited for our inner circle, and there is no telling if there is availability at this very moment. For those who are serious about joining our inner circle, the best advice to get accepted into our program is to join the Million Dollar Plan coaching group at http://milliondollarplan.net and we will notify you on our inner circle availability.

The purpose of this book was to inspire and give ideas on how you can expand your business by leveraging technology. There is no 'one-size-fits-all' business plan or marketing plan; however, do what others have done before you and find inspiration in how other entrepreneurs are creating success in their businesses. If you choose to continue learning from me, find me on social media and let's connect. But don't just sit around and listen, jump into conversation because I want to hear about you and your dreams.

If you take no further action, that is OK too. I understand that building an online presence is not important to everyone, but I thank you sincerely for taking the time to read my book. For those of you who are excited and ready to go to the next level, come join me this journey and we will continue to grow together. Every step that I take in my business is documented online, and I give workshops and live training that can help you along the way.

There are more books planned for the future, and more value that I can provide that extend beyond these pages. The next step is yours, and I look forward to hearing more about you and your business in our coaching group and also through social media.

It doesn't matter who you are, where you come from, who your parents are, what level of education you have, or your previous experiences in life. Believe in yourself, work hard, and know that you have greatness inside of you. We are all special and we have the ability to achieve anything we set our minds to. Get started building your dreams today and know there is nothing holding you back.

MASTERING THE MILLION DOLLAR PLAN

To learn more about the Mastering Group visit: http://milliondollarplan.net

SCALEUP ACADEMY

Building technology to scale a business can be confusing and overwhelming to most people, and because of this, Matthew has created ScaleUP Academy, a website dedicated to training entrepreneurs on what is working in marketing and advertising. Follow along in video training workshops how to set up web pages that convert traffic to leads, and follow along in the building of sales funnels to turn leads into sales. Learn the strategies that are working today in online marketing and join in the discussions online through the groups.

To learn more about ScaleUP Academy, visit: http://scaleupacademy.com

SCALEUP MEDIA

This book was published through ScaleUP Media, founded by Matthew J. Ganzak. The foundation of this business was built on Matthew's mantra - test everything, track the results and report the findings. Through this mantra, he has created several training websites that document and outline exactly what has been tested and the results of the test. ScaleUP Media was founded on the same principals to assist future authors to follow in Matthew's footsteps to self-publish their first book.

To learn more about ScaleUP Media, visit: http://scaleupmedia.com.

SCALEUP CONSULTING

Matthew has been consulting for companies for over a decade in a dozen different industries. His consulting experience is the backbone of the training and this book is a further step towards scaling the business. Matthew's time is limited, and the consulting services are only available to a select few businesses throughout the year. Through the evolution of ScaleUP Consulting, there is a certification program on the horizon (if not already launched). The certification is available to consultants who are looking to grow their consulting business.

For more information, visit http://scaleupconsulting.com

SCALEUP 360

Matthew has live workshops that are planned throughout the year, and you can learn more about these live events coming up.

For more information, visit http://scaleup360.com

Matthew J. Ganzak is founder of several successful websites, a podcaster, author and founder of ScaleUP Academy, ScaleUP Media, ScaleUP 360 and ScaleUP Consulting; websites that are dedicated to helping entrepreneurs start, grow and scale their businesses online. He teaches members how to create information products, sell books, and grow their online influence. Through his marketing efforts, Matt has sold millions of dollars in products and services worldwide, has been featured on television and on popular blogs. His focus is to help entrepreneurs create successful businesses, and is dedicated to creating valuable education.

To learn more about Matthew, visit http://mattganzak.com